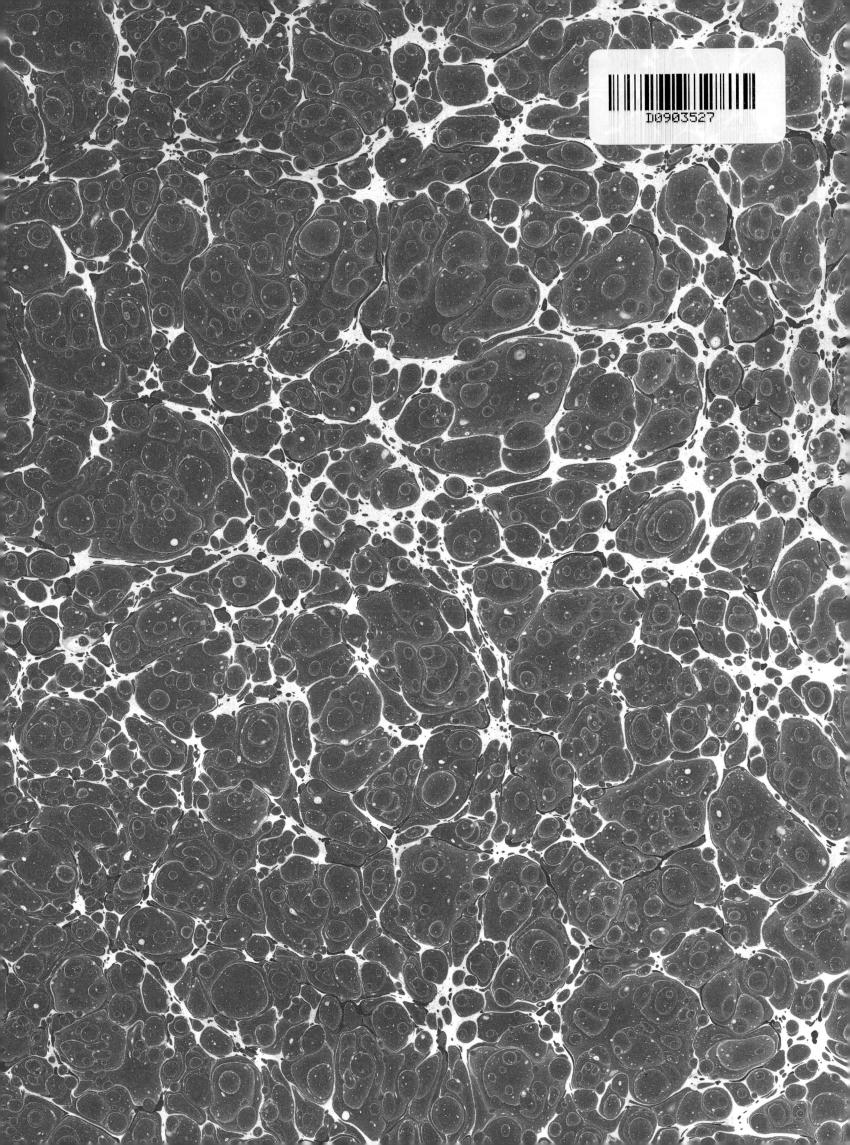
D0903527

# BASEBALL TREASURES

## Memorabilia from the National Pastime

Douglas Congdon-Martin

John Kashmanian

*Schiffer Publishing Ltd*

77 Lower Valley Road, Atglen, PA 19310

## Dedications

I dedicate this book to my wife, Ann,
and my children, Lauren and John,
whose patience and support have made this project possible.
And to all those who in some manner have helped me
build my collection over the years.

John Kashmanian

I wish to dedicate this book
to my son, Joshua,
who loves the game.

Douglas Congdon-Martin

## Acknowledgements

The authors wish to thank the many people who have contributed to this volume. Their willingness to share the treasures of their collections have made this work as complete as it is.

Mike Brown gave up a day's work and generously welcomed us into his New Jersey home. We spent many enjoyable hours photographing his collection, though, in fact, we only touched the surface.

In the same way, we spent a day with Ted Patterson of Baltimore. Like Mike, Ted has an extensive collection that he has been building for many years. As a sportscaster he has had an unusual access to the players and the game, which has contributed to the wonderful variety of baseball memorabilia he has amassed.

Others who have helped include Tom Grey of Winston-Salem, North Carolina, Peg Osborne of Chicago, Dennis O'Brien and George Goehring of Baltimore, Baldwin's Book Barn of West Chester, Pennsylvania, the Manchester, New Hampshire Historical Society, John Delph, Mark Rucker, and Hy Brown.

To bring all of this together is no little task. It can only be done with the help of a talented supportive team. We especially thank Ellen (Sue) Taylor of the Schiffer team who designed the book and Kate Dooner who recorded much of the information.

Copyright © 1992 by Douglas Congdon-Martin and John Kashmanian
Library of Congress Catalog Number: 92-83775.

All rights reserved. No part of this work may be reproduced or used in any forms or by any means—graphic, electronic or mechanical, including photocopying or information storage and retrieval systems—without written permission from the copyright holder.

Printed in the United States of America.
ISBN: 0-88740-492-8

Published by Schiffer Publishing, Ltd.
77 Lower Valley Road
Atglen, PA 19310
Please write for a free catalog.
This book may be purchased from the publisher.
Please include $2.95 postage.
Try your bookstore first.

We are interested in hearing from authors with book ideas on related subjects.

# Contents

Willie Mays, Professional Model WM, youth's baseball glove, c. 1952. Following the integration of baseball, manufacturers began to seek the endorsements of black players. This is one of the earliest products to carry Mays' name. *From the Congdon-Martin Collection.*

This two-page spread from *Frank Leslie's Illustrated Newspaper*, November 4, 1865, shows the "Great Base Ball Match" between the Atlantic and Eckford Clubs of Brooklyn, at the Union Base Ball Grounds, Brooklyn, Oct. 13, 1865. It includes portraits of the leading players of the principal clubs of New York, Brooklyn, and Newark. Across the bottom are Thomas Dakin-Putnam, B. Hannegan-Union, Chas. E. Thomas-Eureka, A.J. Bixby-Eagle, Dr. Wm. H. Bell-Eclectic, Mort Rogers-Resolute, Thos. Miller-Empire, S.C. Leland-Enterprise, Robt. Manly-Star, John Crum-Eckford, and J. Seaver Page-Active.

At the center of the top is James Creighton of the Excelsior Club, one of the first players to accept pay for playing. His fame grew into legendary status when he was fatally wounded in the act of hitting a home run in a game between the Excelsiors and the Union Club of Morrisania on October 14, 1862. He died four days later of a ruptured bladder. The other players at the top of the engraving include Dan'l Manson-Mystic Yorkville, Joseph Leggett-Excelsior, T.G. Vancott-Gotham, James W. Davis-Knickerbocker, John Wildey-Mutual, and P.O. Brien-Atlantic. To the left of the game is T.C. Voorhis, President of the Base Ball Convention, and to the right is an early image of Henry Chadwick, generally acknowledged as one of the "Fathers of Baseball." *From the Kashmanian Collection.*

Invitation to join the Enterprise Base Ball Club dated July 30, 1860. Before contracts, base ball clubs were like men's clubs with membership extended by invitation. 5" x 8". *From the Kashmanian Collection.*

# Chapter 1
# *Transcending the Years*

In the truest sense of the word, this is not a history, though historians of baseball will be fascinated by the artifacts that fill these pages. It is more akin to finding a trunk in your grandparent's attic packed with a lifetime of memories. There is a sense of curiosity as you leaf through the old photographs, wondering who this person was and looking for family resemblances. And there is an almost palpable feeling of history, a connectedness that transcends the years.

The *Baseball Treasures* on these pages have that same power. The photographs take us back to the earliest years of the game, giving flesh to the statistics and stories that baseball fans love so much. As you look into the player's eyes you can find the same intensity, competitiveness, and joy that you will find in the eyes of today's little or big leaguer. The game connects them. It is the bloodline that ties one generation to another.

This hand-tinted Reward of Merit was given by school teachers to reward achievement. Dating to the 1840s, it is one of the earliest images of baseball known to exist. 2.75" x 6.5". Printed by the N. Orp Co. *From the Kashmanian Collection.*

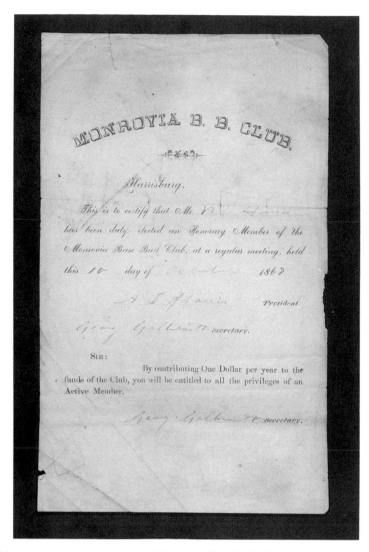

Honorary membership to the Monrovia Base Ball Club, October 10, 1867. Harrisburg, Pennsylvania. Bestowed on W. Harris. *From the Kashmanian Collection.*

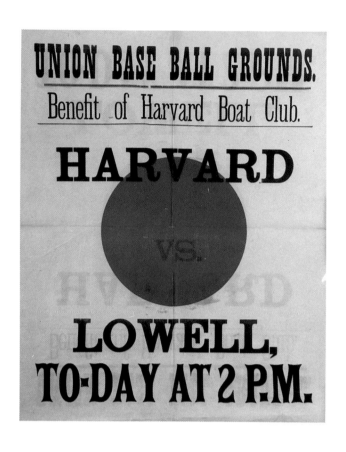

Broadside of a game played between Harvard and Lowell on October 26, 1869. Lowell was a Boston team that took the name of one of its founding members, John A. Lowell. 19" x 24". *From the Kashmanian Collection.*

Silk ribbon for the Athletic Base Ball Club of Philadelphia, c. early 1870s. 3.25" x 5". *From the Kashmanian Collection.*

The players are not the only ones linked by this game. So are the fans. Indeed, if the "kranks" had not been so smitten by the game, many of these treasures would have been lost long ago. From the earliest days there was something about baseball that begged to be preserved, a sense that something historic was happening on the grassy fields. So people bought carte de visite or cabinet photographs of the players and cherished them like family images. They hung team pictures on their walls. They tucked scorecards and programs into drawers, perhaps retrieving them now and again to prod the memory of a particular game, or letting them safely lie to be rediscovered by a future generation.

Because of this drive to preserve a bit of history, baseball fans have created a material culture that is unrivaled by any other sport. Their appetite for mementos, souvenirs, books and magazines, and even home decor and accessories with a baseball theme has remained insatiable. It did not take an advertising genius to see the marketing potential in all of this.

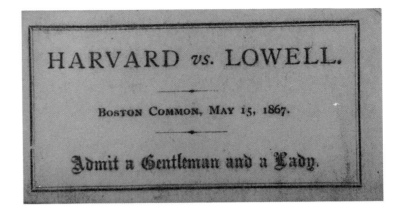

Base ball ticket to see Harvard vs. Lowell, Boston Common, May 15, 1867. It admitted a gentleman and a lady. 3.25" x 2". *From the Kashmanian Collection.*

Base ball ticket to see Harvard vs. Lowell, Olympic Grounds, Medford, Massachusetts, June 1, 1867. *From the Kashmanian Collection.*

Cover of the *New England Base Ballist* , a very early base ball newspaper. Aug. 13, 1868, Vol 1, No. 2, published in Boston. Featured on the cover Is John A. Lowell, organizer of the Lowell Base Ball Club of Boston, one of the prominent teams of the era. The title of the article on page one contains one of the earliest references to baseball as "the National Game." *From the Kashmanian Collection.*

Baseball players soon found their images on tobacco cards, trolley signs, cigar bands, and on boxes for everything from cereal to underwear. All of these and more have found their way into the baseball treasure chest.

Why this fascination with a game? One of the reasons is its accessibility. Long before baseball was played by professionals, it was a popular game in the towns and cities of America. In New England, town ball was a welcome diversion during breaks in the interminable town meetings. The whole town could play, with a limitless number on players each team. As the game developed it became a little less chaotic. Team sizes were limited and rules were developed, yet the game was still a sport for amateurs. Wherever a group of children, an open field, a stick, and a ball were found together, the ingredients were in place for an afternoon of baseball.

The participatory nature of baseball was true for adults as well, but with growing up spontaneity fades and the need to organize the world takes on greater importance. So, by the

Ticket to Alaska Base Ball Club Annual Soiree, Dec. 14, 1869, Brooklyn, New York. *From the Kashmanian Collection.*

Tintype of an unidentified player. c. 1875. *From the Kashmanian Collection.*

Philadelphia Athletics on the front page of *The Daily Graphic,* a New York newspaper, July 14, 1874. In the center is Dick McBride, and clockwise from the top center are Wes Fisler, Al Reach, John McMullin, Mike McGeary, Count Gedney, John Clapp, Cap Anson, Count Sensenderfer, Ezra Sutton, and Joe Battin. 12″ x 19″. *From the Kashmanian Collection.*

Metal statue, bat missing, Müller, New York, patent 1868. 10″. *From the Kashmanian Collection.*

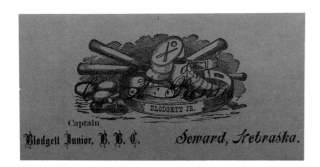

Calling card of C.A. Bemis of Blodgett Junior Base Ball Club. Seward, Nebraska. *From the Kashmanian Collection.*

$10,000 stock certificate for the Olympic Base Ball Club of Washington, D.C. incorporated in 1870. It is signed by A.G. Mills, president and is dated December, 1870. 10" x 7". *From the Kashmanian Collection.*

time Alexander Cartwright wrote down rules for his Knickerbocker team in 1845, the amateur game of baseball was being dominated by clubs. These baseball clubs were organized much as other men's social clubs of the day, and made up what Warren Goldstein calls "The Base Ball Fraternity" (*Playing for Keeps*, p. 17). They had officers, constitutions and rules, membership dues, and regular meetings. Their size could range from small enough to field one team to large enough to field three or four teams, ranked according to their ability. The "first nine" would be have the best players on its roster, while the "muffin nine" would be have the least skilled players, who often played more for fun than competition.

Indeed the baseball clubs involved much fun and socializing. Large collations and soirees were in order when a visiting team came to play a match. They were often met by brass bands and given a rousing escort to the playing field. Afterwards they were treated with food, entertainment, and good will. As Goldstein tells it, "Postgame 'ceremonies' were in fact rituals by which the recently divided and occasionally disordered ball field was reclaimed in the name of the baseball fraternity and its standard of good fellowship." (*Playing for Keeps*, p. 41.)

As the clubs developed during the 1850s and 1860s, the evolution of the baseball professional began. Despite rules of the National Association of Base Ball Players prohibiting the paying of players, it was a common practice. Better players were sought after by the clubs and moving from club to club was frequent. Sometimes the move was motivated by player's

On the letterhead of the Providence Base Ball Association, this is an invitation for the Mayor of Providence to attend a reception honoring the Providence Grays Base Ball team. They had won the championship in 1884. Color engraved paper, 8.5" x 11". *From the Kashmanian Collection.*

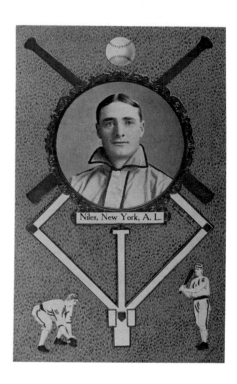

Certificate of shares owned in the Boston Base Ball Association (Red Stockings), dated Nov. 19, 1873. *From the Kashmanian Collection.*

Harry Niles of New York, American League, 1908. Marked TR Co., on back. The Rose Co., 1909. 3.5″ x 5.5″. *From the Kashmanian Collection.*

1880s die-cut figures of base ball players in uniforms of teams of the period, assembled with team names written underneath each. 2.25″ each. Clockwise from top: Indianapolis, Chicago, Boston, Brooklyn, Philadelphia, St. Louis, Pittsburgh, and New York. *From the Kashmanian Collection.*

desire to be part of a better team, but often they moved because of financial opportunities. In the year following the end of Civil War the number of teams more than doubled and baseball spread to seven new states (*Playing for Keeps*, p. 72). Players from the established teams of the east were much sought after by these new teams.

This great expansion of baseball put new stresses on the game. The National Association, originating from a time when the game was simpler and gentler, felt its authority and power gradually erode. It was not up to the new demands and admitted as much in 1868 when it acknowledged that baseball should be divided in "two classes," professional and amateur. In 1869 the Cincinnati Red Stocking were formed as the first admittedly professional base ball team. In 1870 the National Association held its last convention.

While there are some interesting artifacts that predate the rise of professionalism, most of what has come to us is from the professional era. As clubs became businesses they became subject to the laws of the marketplace. Their health and prosperity was directly tied to the number of fans who paid to see the games. The clubs worked hard to reach the public. Players were promoted as heroes and teams took on the aura of armies defending the civic pride of the community. The game was touted as the perfect family entertainment and well-suited to a woman's delicate sensitivities; much effort went into keeping the sport true to this ideal. Newspapers became the clarions of the sport, and the writings of Henry Chadwick and other early sports journalists inflamed the public's interest in the game and in its players.

It did not take long for others to jump on the bandwagon. Photographers began to produce carte de visite and cabinet photographs of players and teams to sell to fans anxious to have some memento of their favorites. Team photographs were sold in department stores as the perfect piece of home decor. Advertisers of tobacco, candy, and alcohol began to capitalize on baseball's growing popularity to market their goods. A whole industry developed around creating scorecards, souvenirs, pennants, and other mementoes of the game.

Jimmy Collins, Philadelphia Athletics, American League, 1908. Hall of Fame, 1945. The Rose Co., 1909. Embossed, 3.5" x 5.5". *From the Kashmanian Collection.*

Sam Crawford, Detroit, American League, 1903-1917. Hall of Fame, 1957. The Rose Co., 1909. Embossed, 3.5" x 5.5". *From the Kashmanian Collection.*

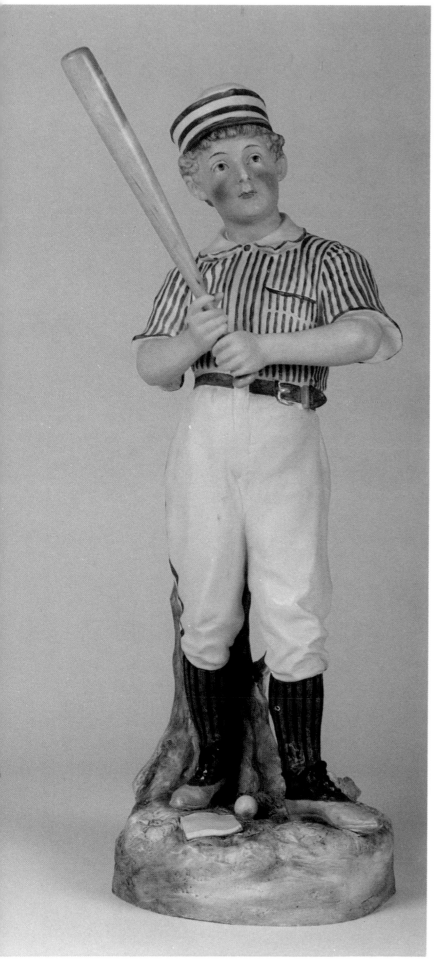

German bisque batter, circa 1880s, made for export to the U.S. These figures came in different sizes, of which these are the tallest known. Geschuetzt Gesetzlioh DEP. 16″ x 6″. The bat is not original. *Courtesy of Mike Brown.*

German bisque outfielder. *Courtesy of Mike Brown.*

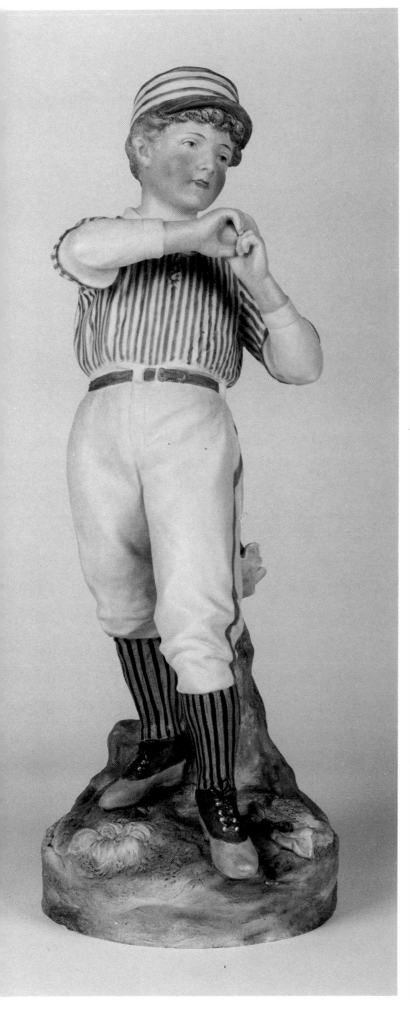

German bisque pitcher. *Courtesy of Mike Brown.*

German bisque infielder. *Courtesy of Mike Brown.*

"Baseball" Published by L. Prang & Co., Boston. Henry Sandham, artist. Copyright 1897. 17" x 23". *From the Kashmanian Collection.*

Something about the game begs to be memorialized. The drama of victory and defeat, of human excellence and human error, of strategy and chance are played out on a field of green. A magical, paradoxical interaction happens. The fans identify so strongly with the players that they are vicariously playing the game themselves, feeling the same adrenalin flow, the same muscle flex and stretch, the same exhilaration at victory, and the same disappointment at defeat. Simultaneously, they are so in awe of the skill and grace, the grit and charisma of their heroes, that the ball park becomes a temple and they are supplicants at its rail.

It is no surprise, then, that the game takes a special place in history that far exceeds its real value in worldly terms. The artifacts that fill this book, and the trunks and shelves of collectors, have endured simply because they are tangible evidence. They trigger stories and memories that can be drawn upon again and again, each time awakening some of the original feeling and power. We hope you enjoy and cherish them as much as we do.

# Chapter 2
# *Hero Images*

Warren Goldstein makes a good argument for the connection of early baseball teams to the volunteer firefighting companies of the day, suggesting that many of the companies had baseball teams associated with them (*Playing for Keeps*, page 28 ff.). The physical evidence is convincing. The uniforms were nearly identical. Indeed the advertising of Peck & Snyder, the foremost manufacturer of sporting equipment in the mid-1800s, shows a fireman's uniform right next to the baseball uniforms. Beyond the uniforms, the social traditions of parades, soirees, and collations that surrounded early baseball games find an almost exact parallel in the festivities that took place when one fire company visited another.

The Mutuals of New York, an early baseball team, were founded in 1857 by the Mutual Hook and Ladder Company No. 1, and time and time again the names of baseball team echoed the names of fire companies: Knickerbocker, Atlantic, Invincible, Perseverance. Goldstein concludes that, "If not all baseball club names had antecedents in fire companies, nearly all fire-company names were picked up by baseball clubs."

Whatever the case, the public held firefighters and baseball players in similar awe. They were heroes of the day, and this is reflected in the early images that were made of them. Most of the photographs we have of the early baseball players and firefighters were taken in the years following the Civil War. This was the age of Mathew Brady, Timothy O'Sullivan and other pioneer photographers who followed the action and the warriors in the conflict. As they made photographs of soldiers that could be sent home to loved ones, they developed a style of heroic portraiture that is seen in the early, full-figure images of ball players. The photographs of groups of Civil War soldiers used poses that are remarkably similar to the team pictures of the early teams.

Many of the young men in the earliest photos fought in the war. When they returned, baseball experienced a significant growth in popularity. After such a brutal conflict, one imagines that there was a deep sense of relief and joy as the confrontations moved from the battlefields to the ball fields. But baseball was also a way of continuing the excitement of soldiering into civilian life.

Boyd Packer, Williamsport Base Ball Club, carte de visite, c. 1867, Williamsport, Pennsylvania. R.C. Chase & Co., Photographers, Williamsport, Pennsylvania. 2.5″ x 4″. *From the Kashmanian Collection.*

For many of the combatants, the Civil War was their first exposure to a world outside of their farm or village. They experienced first hand the breadth of the country and the diversity of its people. And, despite the mortal danger they faced, they knew something of the exhilaration of being part of a team and going into competition. The war also represented the first exposure many of them had had to the game of baseball. It was played in camp as a way of whiling away the hours between conflicts with the enemy. There is one famous print of Union prisoners in a Salisbury, N.C. prison camp playing ball in 1862.

With the end of the war, these soldiers scattered to the far corners of the land, and with them they carried the enthusiasm for baseball that would make it truly a "national" game.

Carte de visite of unknown player. 4″ x 2.5″. *From the Kashmanian Collection.*

Carte de visite of unknown player. 4″ x 2.5″. *From the Kashmanian Collection.*

# Player Photographs

"Representatives of Professional Baseball in America." Lithograph by Root & Tinker, Tribune Bldg. New York, 1884. 26" x 20.5". At the bottom are Adrian Anson, Joe Start, Pop Snyder. From third to first base around the outside are Harry Stovey, Art Whitney, Guy Hecker, Charlie Bennett, Buck Ewing, John Morrill, Tim Keefe, Dan Brouthers, Pat Deasley. In the center are A.G. Spalding, A.G. Mills, Harry Wright, and N.E. Young. *From the Kashmanian Collection.*

Jonas L. Clinton, manager, is among the cabinet photographs of the members of Manchester "Manchesters" Base Ball Club of New Hampshire, a semi-professional team from the early 1880s. All are by Wallace Photography, Manchester, New Hampshire, 8.25″ x 4″. *From the Kashmanian Collection.*

Theodore J. Scheffler, center field. Played for Detroit in 1888 and for Rochester in 1890. *From the Kashmanian Collection.*

John J. "Handsome Jack" Carney, first base. Played for Washington (1889), Buffalo and Cleveland (Players League, 1890), and Cincinnati and Milwaukee (American Association). *From the Kashmanian Collection.*

William F. Klusman, second base. Played for Boston (1888) and St. Louis (American Association, 1890). *From the Kashmanian Collection.*

John J. "Chief" Kelty, left fielder. Played for Pittsburgh, 1890. *From the Kashmanian Collection.*

David Coughlin, right fielder. *From the Kashmanian Collection.*

Owen "Spider" Clark, catcher. Played for Washington (1889) and Buffalo (Players League, 1890). Notice the glove on his catching hand. *From the Kashmanian Collection.*

E.J. Doyle, fielder. *From the Kashmanian Collection.*

# The Manchester "Manchesters"

William Irwin, pitcher. Played for Cincinnati in the American Association, 1886. *From the Kashmanian Collection.*

John J. "Rooney" Sweeney, Catcher. Played for Baltimore (American Association, 1883), Baltimore (Union Association, 1884), and St. Louis (1885). *From the Kashmanian Collection.*

Michael McDermott, pitcher. Mike played for Louisville (American Association, 1889 and National League, 1895-6), and for Cleveland and St. Louis, 1897. *From the Kashmanian Collection.*

John Staib, pitcher. *From the Kashmanian Collection.*

E.W. Ellis, pitcher. *From the Kashmanian Collection.*

John Shoupe, short stop. Played for Troy (1879), St. Louis (American Association, 1882), Washington (Union Association, 1884). *From the Kashmanian Collection.*

Daniel J. "Dan" Mahoney, catcher. Played for Cincinnati (1892) and Washington (1895). *From the Kashmanian Collection.*

John Campana and mascot, third base. *From the Kashmanian Collection.*

Cabinet photograph of Mike "King" Kelly, Boston, advertising Old Judge Cigarettes, Goodwin & Co., New York, c. 1887. Hall of Fame, 1945. *From the Kashmanian Collection.*

Charlie Ganzel, catcher, Boston, cabinet photograph, c. 1889. Copyright 1887 Goodwin & Co., New York. *From the Kashmanian Collection.*

Michael "Kid" Madden, pitcher, Boston. Copyright, 1887, Goodwin & Co., New York. 1888. *From the Kashmanian Collection.*

Joe Quinn, second base, Boston. Cabinet photograph, copyright 1888, Goodwin & Co., New York. 1888. *From the Kashmanian Collection.*

Frank Chance, Chicago National, cabinet studio photo from *Sporting Life*, Philadelphia. Black and white, c. 1909-1912. Hall of Fame, 1946. *From the Kashmanian Collection.*

Cabinet photograph of John Sowders, pitcher, Boston, issued by Old Judge Cigarettes, Goodwin & Co., 1888. 4.25″ x 6.5. *From the Kashmanian Collection.*

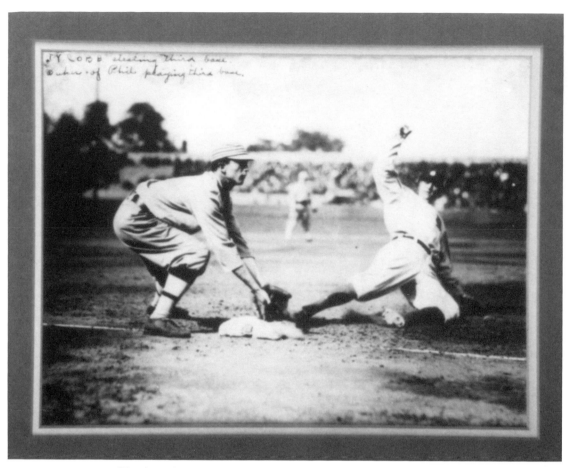

Photograph of Ty Cobb stealing base with Frank "Home Run" Baker, Philadelphia, on third. Both Cobb and Baker are in the Hall of Fame. 9.75" x 7.75". *From the Kashmanian Collection.*

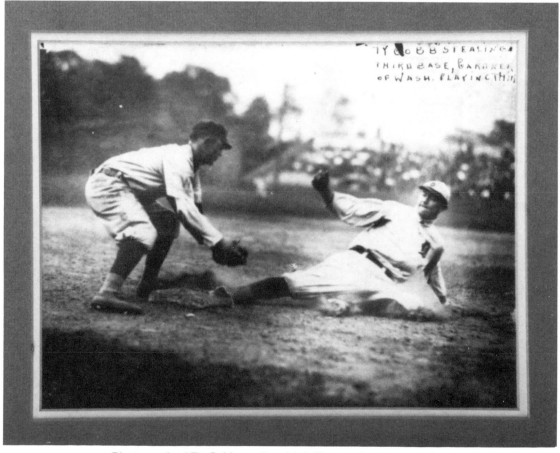

Photograph of Ty Cobb stealing third. The caption suggests that "Gardner" of Washington is on third. Since no Gardner played for Washington during this time, it must be another Washington third baseman. 9.75" x 7.75". *From the Kashmanian Collection.*

Photo of Ty Cobb stealing home. 9.75″ x 7.75″. *From the Kashmanian Collection.*

Grover Alexander, Philadelphia National, 1911-1917. Photograph by Paul Thompson. Hall of Fame, 1938. *Courtesy of Mike Brown.*

Chief Bender, Philadelphia American (Athletics), 1903-1914.
Photograph by Paul Thompson. Hall of Fame, 1953. *Courtesy of Mike Brown.*

**Opposite page:**
Dave Bancroft, a member of the New York Giants. Photograph by Paul Thompson. *Courtesy of Mike Brown.*

Roger Bresnahan, Chicago National (Cubs), 1913-1915.
Photograph by Paul Thompson. Hall of Fame, 1945. *Courtesy of Mike Brown.*

Fred Clarke, Manager, Pittsburgh Nationals (Pirates), 1900-1915. Photograph by Paul Thompson. Hall of Fame, 1945. *Courtesy of Mike Brown.*

Ty Cobb, Detroit Tigers, 1905-1926. Photograph by Paul Thompson. Hall of Fame, 1936. *Courtesy of Mike Brown.*

Frank Chance, New York American, 1913-1914. Photograph by Paul Thompson. Hall of Fame, 1946. *Courtesy of Mike Brown.*

Stan Covaleski of Cleveland, 1916-1924, proud hero of the 1920 World Series, when he won three games against Brooklyn with three five-hitters. Photograph by Paul Thompson. Hall of Fame, 1969. *Courtesy of Mike Brown.*

Sam Crawford, Detroit Tigers, 1903-1917. Photograph by Paul Thompson. Hall of Fame, 1957. *Courtesy of Mike Brown.*

Burleigh Grimes, pitcher, Pittsburgh, 1916-1917. Photograph by Paul Thompson. Hall of Fame, 1964. *Courtesy of Mike Brown.*

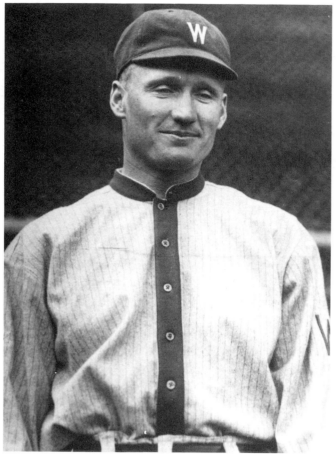

Walter Johnson, pitcher, Washington, 1907-1927. Photograph by Paul Thompson. Hall of Fame, 1936. *Courtesy of Mike Brown.*

William Klem, umpire. Hall of Fame. Photograph by Paul Thompson. *Courtesy of Mike Brown.*

A photograph of Kenesaw Mountain Landis, taken at the 1918 World Series. Photograph by Paul Thompson. *Courtesy of Mike Brown.*

Christy Mathewson, manager at Cincinnati, 1916-1918, making out his batting order. A doctored version of this photo appears on the Christy Mathewson game. Photograph by Paul Thompson. Hall of Fame, 1936. *Courtesy of Mike Brown.*

John McGraw, manager New York Giants, 1902-1932, taking them to nine World Series. Photograph by Paul Thompson. Hall of Fame, 1937. *Courtesy of Mike Brown.*

Edd Roush, Cincinnati, 1917-1926. Photograph by Paul Thompson. Hall of Fame, 1962. *Courtesy of Mike Brown.*

Babe Ruth. The photographer's note on the back reads: "The opposing pitcher commences to get nervous—'Babe' en route to the plate 'Batter Up.'" New York Yankees, 1920-1934. Photograph by Paul Thompson. Hall of Fame, 1936. *Courtesy of Mike Brown.*

Tris Speaker, manager, Cleveland American, 1919-1926. Photograph by Paul Thompson. Hall of Fame, 1937. *Courtesy of Mike Brown.*

Ed Walsh, Chicago American (White Sox), 1904-1916. Photograph by Paul Thompson. Hall of Fame, 1946. *Courtesy of Mike Brown.*

Cy Young with Cleveland, American, near the end of his career, 1909-1911. Photograph by Paul Thompson. Hall of Fame, 1937. *Courtesy of Mike Brown.*

Ruth and President Harding, February 4, 1923. Photograph by Paul Thompson. *Courtesy of Mike Brown.*

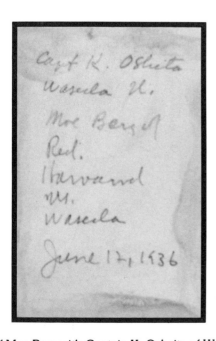

Snapshot of Moe Berg with Captain K. Osheita of Waseda University of Japan. The Japanese team was playing Harvard at Cambridge, Massachusetts on June 12, 1936. In the years leading up to World War II, Berg was a spy for the U.S., using his baseball fame to gain access to Japan. On tours of Japan he took photographs which were used by American intelligence operations. *From the Kashmanian Collection.*

# Player Postcards

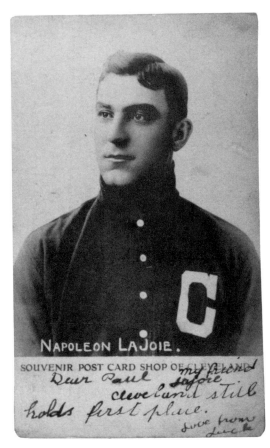

Souvenir post card of Napoleon Lajoie, Cleveland, 1905. Hall of Fame, 1937. 3.25″ x 5.75″. *From the Kashmanian Collection.*

Cy Young pitching for the Boston Red Sox at age 42. Copyrighted and published by A.C. Williams, 1908. 3.5″ x 5.5″. *From the Kashmanian Collection.*

1907 Postal card of Tyrus "Ty" Cobb of Royston, Georgia. From Detroit Seamless Steel Tubes Co., Detroit, Michigan. 5.5″ x 3.25″. *From the Kashmanian Collection.*

Embossed post card for John Anderson, Chicago, American League, 1908. The Rose Co., 1909. 3.5″ x 5.5″. *From the Kashmanian Collection.*

Red Dooin, Philadelphia, National League, 1902-1914. The Rose Co., 1909. Embossed, 3.5″ x 5.5″. *From the Kashmanian Collection.*

Embossed card for Patsy Flaherty, Boston, National League, 1907-1908, 1911. The Rose Co., 1909. 3.5″ x 5.5″. *From the Kashmanian Collection.*

Frank Corridon, Philadelphia, National League, 1905-1909. The Rose Co., 1909. Embossed, 3.5″ x 5.5″. *From the Kashmanian Collection.*

Embossed card for Charlie Jones, St. Louis, American League, 1908. The Rose Co., 1909. 3.5″ x 5.5″. *From the Kashmanian Collection.*

Bill Sweeney, Boston, National League, 1907-1913. The Rose Co., 1909. Embossed, 3.5″ x 5.5″. *From the Kashmanian Collection.*

Embossed card for Ed Killian, pitcher, Detroit, American League, 1904-1910. The Rose Co., 1909. 3.5″ x 5.5″. *From the Kashmanian Collection.*

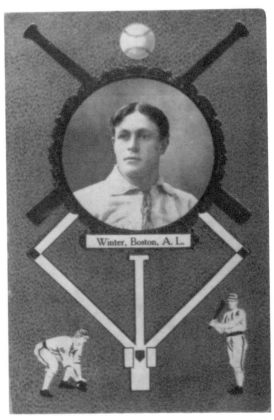

George Winter, Boston, American League, 1901-1908. Marked TR Co., on back. The Rose Co., 1909. 3.5″ x 5.5″. *From the Kashmanian Collection.*

Boston Red Sox catcher, Hick Cady, 1912-1917. Underwood and Underwood, New York. 3.5″ x 5.5″. *From the Kashmanian Collection.*

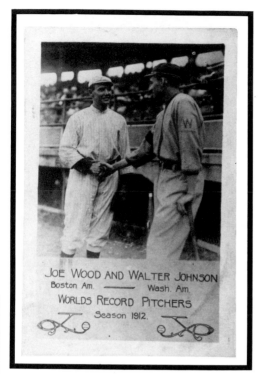

Joe Wood, Boston American, and Walter Johnson, Washington American, "World's Record Pitchers," 1912. The Photo Art Shop, Swampscott, Massachusetts. 3.5″ x 5.5″. *From the Kashmanian Collection.*

New York Giants pitcher Rube Marquard, 1908-1915. Hall of Fame, 1971. Underwood & Underwood, New York. 3.5″ x 5.5″. *From the Kashmanian Collection.*

Boston Red Sox pitcher, Smokey Joe Wood, 1908-1915. Underwood & Underwood, New York. 3.5″ x 5.5″. *From the Kashmanian Collection.*

Christy Mathewson, pitcher for the New York Giants, 1900-1916. Hall of Fame, 1936. Underwood & Underwood, New York. 3.5″ x 5.5″. *From the Kashmanian Collection.*

TRIS SPEAKER
STAR OUTFIELDER AND CHAMPION
BATTER OF THE RED SOX
BOSTON AMERICAN SERIES

Tris Speaker, on one of the *Boston Sunday American's* series of post cards, c. 1912. 3.5″ x 5″. *From the Kashmanian Collection.*

Advertising post card for J.I. Case T.M. Co., Lansing Michigan. In the car with Barney Oldfield, the pioneer race car driver, is Joe Tinker of the Chicago Cubs, being given his first driving lesson in the new Case Car. 3.5″ x 5.5″. *From the Kashmanian Collection.*

Harold Lloyd

Babe Ruth post card, 3.5″ x 5.5″. *From the Kashmanian Collection.*

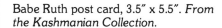

BABE RUTH [U.S.A.]
WORLD'S CHAMPION BASEBALL
PLAYER

A German post card for Harold Lloyd and Babe Ruth, 1928. They were in a movie together. Published by Ross. *From the Kashmanian Collection.*

Hazen S. "Ki Ki" Cuyler advertising post card for Charles Denby Cigars, c. 1932. 3.5″ x 5.5″. Facsimile signature on front. Hall of Fame, 1968. *From the Kashmanian Collection.*

HEAD-QUARTERS

# BOSTON BASE BALL CLUB,

18 BOYLSTON STREET,

Boston, December 5th 1873.

H. A. McGlenen Esq.

Dear Sir.

At the Annual meeting of the Boston Base Ball Association held at their club rooms No. 591 Washington Street on Wednesday afternoon December 3rd, the Board of Directors acknowledged themselves under great obligations to you for the assistance you rendered in making the club a financial success, which the report of the Treasurer showing a balance on hand of $767.93 is sufficient proof thereof, it was "Voted! That the thanks of the Association be extended to H. A. McGlenen for his generous and invaluable services in behalf of the Association during the past season."

Yours Respectfully,
Harry Wright
Clerk.

Hand written letter by Harry Wright, the Boston Base Ball Club,
December 5th, 1873. *From the Kashmanian Collection.*

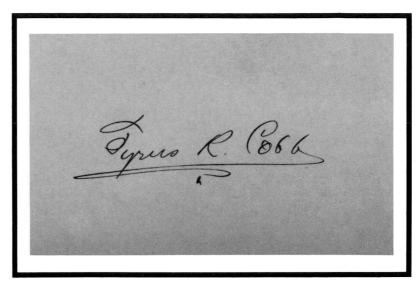

Autograph of Ty Cobb. 3″ x 5″. *From the Kashmanian Collection.*

Autographed photograph of Ty Cobb, signed Feb. 5, 1961. 6.25″ x 10″. *From the Kashmanian Collection.*

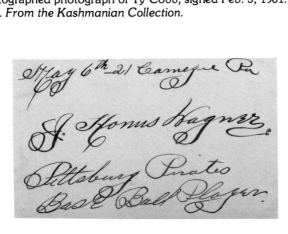

Autograph of Honus Wagner, May 6, 1921. Written four years after his last season, he identifies himself as simply, "Base Ball Player." 3″ x 5″. *From the Kashmanian Collection.*

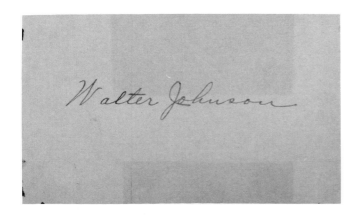

Autograph of Walter Johnson. 3″ x 5″. *From the Kashmanian Collection.*

Autographed photo of Hugh Jennings, 1912, manager of the Detroit Tigers. In 1912 he had one at bat for Detroit. Hall of Fame, 1945. 7″ x 9″. *From the Kashmanian Collection.*

Autograph of Napoleon Lajoie. 3″ x 5″. *From the Kashmanian Collection.*

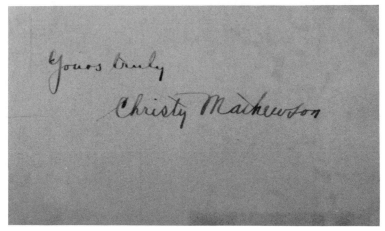

Autograph of Christy Mathewson. 3″ x 5″. *From the Kashmanian Collection.*

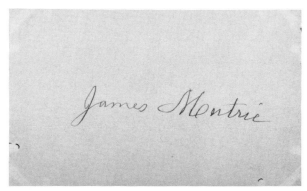

Autograph of James Mutrie, manager New York 1883-1891. 3″ x 5″. *From the Kashmanian Collection.*

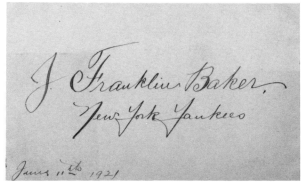

1921 autograph of J. Franklin "Home Run" Baker, New York Yankees. 3″ x 5″. *From the Kashmanian Collection.*

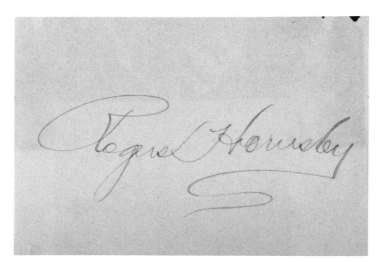

Autograph of Rogers Hornsby. 3″ x 5″. *From the Kashmanian Collection.*

Autograph of George H. Sisler. 3″ x 5″. *From the Kashmanian Collection.*

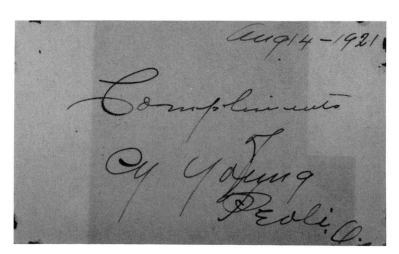

1921 autograph of Cy Young. 3″ x 5″. *From the Kashmanian Collection.*

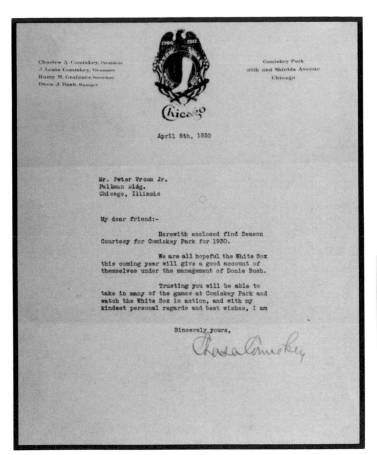

Letter from Charles A. Comiskey, President, Chicago White Sox, to Peter Vroom, Jr., dated April 5, 1930, and referring to enclosed season's tickets for 1930, courtesy of the Park. *From the Kashmanian Collection.*

Autographed photo of Lou Gehrig. Dated 1938. Hall of Fame, 1939. 7.5″ x 9.5″. *From the Kashmanian Collection.*

Autographed photograph of Mel Ott. George Burke, photographer. 6″ x 4″. *From the Kashmanian Collection.*

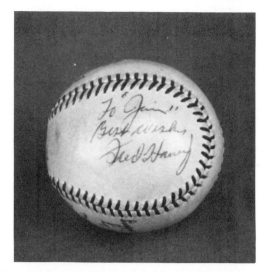

Same ball, autograph of Fred Haney, manager of the Milwaukee Braves.

The first ball thrown out at the 1958 World Series, by James Crusinberry, former Chicago Tribune writer and one of the founders of Base Ball Writers Association in 1908. Signed by Casey Stengel, manager of New York, and Fred Haney, manager of Milwaukee. *From the Kashmanian Collection.*

Autograph of Casey Stengel, manager of the New York Yankees.

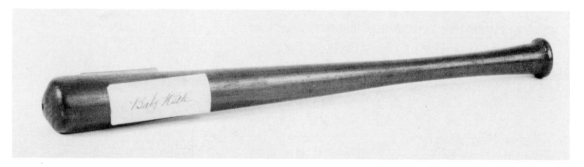

Souvenir of 1927 World Series with a Babe Ruth autograph added to front. 16.5" long. *Courtesy of Ted Patterson.*

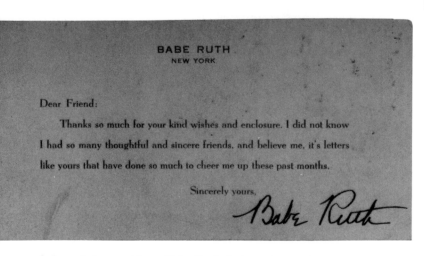

Acknowledgement from Babe Ruth during a hospital stay, sent out in response to letters from well wishers. 7" x 3.5". *From the Kashmanian Collection.*

# Chapter 3
# *From Armies to Teams*

As stated earlier the images of early baseball teams on these pages closely resemble the photographs of Civil War units taken by Brady and other photographic pioneers. The formal poses, the "weapons" laid at the feet, the uniforms, and the demeanor of the players reflect the seriousness of purpose and the sense of confidence these young men possessed.

These images were made principally for purchase by fans. They are a reflection of the growing popularity that baseball was achieving as a spectator sport. In earlier times, sports events were rough and tumble events that appealed to the men of the community. One of the innovations of baseball was its civility. Early on it was seen as "suitable" entertainment for women, and much effort went into keeping it that way. Indeed, in 1876, when William Ambrose Hulbert called the meeting that would establish the National League, one of the motivations was to put an end to the bad behavior of players and fans alike, and restore the respectability that would bring the public back in greater numbers. The strategy worked and baseball has continued to be a sport that appeals to a great cross section of fans.

## Team Photographs

Hand-tinted photograph of the 1863 Pasttime Baseball Club. 15.5" x 12". *From the Kashmanian Collection.*

The Knickerbockers of Albany, 1864. They share the same name
as the original Knickerbockers of 1845. The founder of that team,
Alexander Cartwright, established the game that is the model upon
which modern baseball is formed. Published by Wagoner &
McDonald, Albany, New York. The players (left to right): Turner,
J. Lindsley, Umpleby, Bantham, Ford, Corey, Combs, DeWitt,
W.H. Davis, Winne, Bliss, MacDonald, J.S. Hurdis, Gardner, J.C.
Cutler, Lathrop. 19″ x 11″. *From the Kashmanian Collection.*

One of the things that is apparent from the early team
images is that there were no African-American players. In 1858,
players founded the National Association of Base Ball Players.
It helped to standardize the game, and in its early days was
quite instrumental in the development of the game. In the
expansion of baseball following the Civil War its influence
faltered. Questions of representation and eligibility were
debated with vigor in the convention of 1866. The Nominating
Committee which decided on the qualifications of applicants for
membership in the NABBP was in such confusion that it simply
"assumed" that applications were made in "good faith" (*Playing
for Keeps*, page 87 ff.). But on one matter it was not so lenient:
"It is not presumed by your committee," it reported to the
convention, "that any club who have applied are composed of
person of color, or any portion of them; and the
recommendation of your committee in this report are based
upon this view, and they unanimously report against the
admission of any club which may be composed of one or more
colored persons."

Very early on the pattern was set. Even though the demise of
the NABBP was only a few years away, baseball would be a

Carte de Visite, Hudson River Base Ball Club, c. 1865. Photographer, Pope, Newburgh, New York. *From the Kashmanian Collection.*

Considered the first professional baseball team, the Cincinnati Red Stockings Base Ball Club sat for this carte de visite, c. 1869. The Red Stockings did much to promote baseball. They travelled 11,000 miles and won 57 straight games in 1869 (a streak that continued to 92 the following year). Henry Chadwick wrote that "they took their place upon the field, and during the campaign that year they encountered every strong club in the country from Maine to California, and they met with such remarkable success as to make their career in that year noteworthy." The team included Andy Leonard, George Wright, Douglas Allison, Calvin McVey, and Richard Hurley, Charles Sweasy, Fred Waterman, Harry Wright (seated in the middle), Asa Brainard, and Charlie Gould. *From the Kashmanian Collection.*

white game for nearly a century. In the years that followed there were a few notable exceptions to the rule. Bud Fowler, Moses Fleetwood Walker and William Welday Walker, Charles Kelly, and Frank Grant were a few of the more than thirty black players who played in the white league before the turn of the century.

Clipper Base Ball Club. Photographer Willis of Milford, state unknown. 4.25" x 6.5". *From the Kashmanian Collection.*

The Mutual Base Ball Club carte de visite trade card, Peck & Snyder, c. 1870. The players: standing (left to right): Candy Nelson, Phoney Martin, Marty Swandell, Dave Eggler; seated (left to right): Everett Mills, John Hatfield, Charlie Mills, Rynie Wolters, Dan Patterson. *From the Kashmanian Collection.*

The Peck & Snyder advertisement on the opposite side of the Atlantics Base Ball Club photo.

Mills.  Zettlen.  Pearce.  Start.  Smith.  Ferguson.  Crane.  Pratt.  Chapman.

The Atlantics Base Ball Club of Brooklyn carte de visite trade card.
Peck & Snyder, c. 1870. The players (left to right): Charlie Mills,
George Zettlen (sic), Dickey Pearce, Joe Start, Charlie Smith, Bob
(Death to Flying Things) Ferguson, Fred Crane, Tom (?) Pratt, and
Jack Chapman. In addition to having one of the more colorful
nicknames in the history of baseball, Bob Ferguson is also credited
with being the first switch hitter. Dickey Pearce may have invented,
or at least perfected the bunt. With the exception of Chapman the
team dispersed to other clubs with the founding of the National
Association in 1871. *From the Kashmanian Collection.*

The pivotal moment of segregation seems to be a game
between the Chicago White Stockings and the team from
Toledo in 1887. Moses Fleetwood Walker was playing for
Toledo. As the game was about to start, Cap Anson, managing
the Chicago team, yelled from the dugout, "Get that nigger off
the field." He refused to let his team take the field against
Toledo unless Walker left the field. The management of Toledo
called Anson's bluff, and threatened to bring spectators from
the stands to represent Chicago if the White Stockings did not
play. Anson relented and the game was played under protest.
(*"Get that Nigger Off the Field"*, page 13).

But the battle was not over, and Anson, almost
singlehandedly continued to press for the segregation of
baseball. Five years later his club faced George Stovey of
Newark and made the same threat. Outraged by the effrontery,
Stovey pulled himself from the game, refusing to face the White
Stockings. Anson continued his assault. When he learned that
Stovey might join Monte Ward's Giants in the major leagues,
he was enraged and pressured Ward to cancel the deal.
Anson's efforts were finally successful, and major league
baseball was white until 1947.

1870 Philadelphia Athletic Base Ball Club.
10" x 12.5". The players (Clockwise from
the top): F.G. (Fergy) Malone, W.D.
(Wes) Fisler, T.J. (Tom) Pratt, J. (Count)
Sensenderfer, H.C. (Harry) Schafer,
Thomas Berry, George Bechtel, John
Radcliffe, A.J. Reach; center: J.D. (Dick)
McBride. *From the Kashmanian
Collection.*

Photograph of the Grafton Base Ball Club, Grafton, Massachusetts. Photographer: Critcherson, Worcester, c. 1875-80. 11.5″ x 9.5″. *From the Kashmanian Collection.*

Composite team photo Boston Red Stockings, c. 1876. The players (clockwise from top center): George Wright, Jack Manning, Joe "Joseph" Borden, Bill Parks, Jim O'Rourke, Andy Leonard, Harry Schafer, Frank Whitney, Tim McGinley, Tim Murnan (sic); center: Harry Wright. *From the Kashmanian Collection.*

1884 team photo of the Columbus Base Ball team of the American Association. The players: *standing, left to right* Patsy Cahill, Ed Dundon, Fred Carroll, Rudolph Kemmler, Jim Fields, Billy Kuehne; *seated* Fred Mann, Tom Brown, Gus Schmelz, Charles "Pop" Smith, Jim Richmond; *reclining* Frank Mountain, Eddie Morris. As the caption says, Columbus finished second to the New York Mets in the 1884 American Association race. 13.5″ x 10.25″. *From the Kashmanian Collection.*

Troy Base Ball Club, c. 1885, in this cabinet photo, by Z.F. Magill Portraits, Troy, New York. 4.25″ x 6.5″. *From the Kashmanian Collection.*

Cabinet photo of Philadelphia Base Ball Club (National League), advertising Kalamazoo Bats tobacco, 1887. At the center is Harry Wright, who managed in Philadelphia from 1884-1895. Other identifiable players are: (top row) Arthur Irwin (left), George Andrews (3rd from left), James Fogerty (5th from left), Deacon McGuire (right); (seated) James Devlin (2nd from left). Other players included S. Farrar, McLaughlin, J. Mulvey, G. Wood, J. Clements, C. Buffinton, C. Ferguson, C. Bastian, D. Casey. 6.5″ x 4.25″. *From the Kashmanian Collection.*

Excluded from white baseball, African-Americans organized their own baseball teams and leagues. There they developed players and teams that were often skilled enough to defeat their white counterparts. Though several African-American leagues were born, few survived more than a few years. Then, in 1920, Rube Foster managed to create a Negro professional league. With the cooperation of Ban Johnson, founder of the American League, Foster's new league had franchises in Kansas City, Indianapolis, Chicago, Detroit, and St. Louis, in addition to the original American Giants and a traveling team of Cuban All Stars (*"Get that Nigger Off the Field"*, pp. 13 ff.). While never the flourishing success of the white leagues, the Negro League survived the Depression, and continued until the integration of the major leagues had drained it of much of its talent.

Boston Base Ball Club photographic collage, copyright 1889 by G. Waldon Smith. 19″ x 13.5″. *From the Kashmanian Collection.*

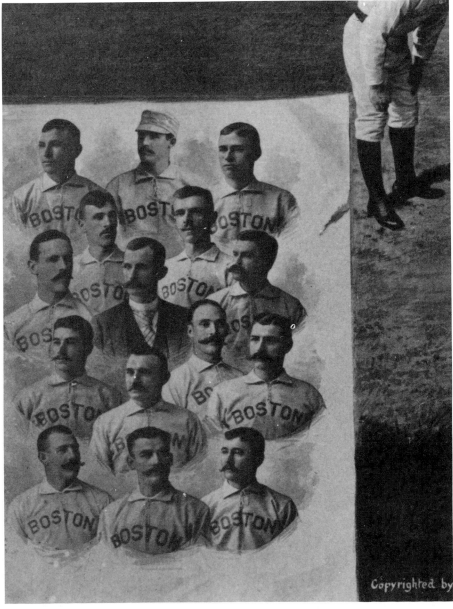

**Opposite page and right:**
Close-up of Jordan Marsh poster above. *From the Kashmanian Collection.*

Advertisement for the lithograph of The Boston Base Ball Club of the 1889 season. The opponents are the New York Base Ball Club with baseman, John M. Ward, and umpire, Wally Fessenden. Copyrighted and published by G. Waldon Smith, Photographer, 145 Tremont St., Boston. Sold exclusively by Jordan, Marsh & Co., Boston. 9.5" x 8". *From the Kashmanian Collection.*

Spalding's All-American Base Ball tour of 1888-89 at the Coliseum in Rome. While Spalding's first tour in 1874 took baseball to Britain, this tour took two teams to Hawaii, Australia, Ceylon, Egypt, Italy, France, England, and Ireland, and helped to spread the interest in baseball to the world community. The photograph was taken on February 28, 1889 by Fratelli D'Alessandro. 21" x 15". *From the Kashmanian Collection.*

Boston Baseball Club, 1888. Copyrighted by G.H. Hastings, 1888. 18" x 13". *From the Kashmanian Collection.*

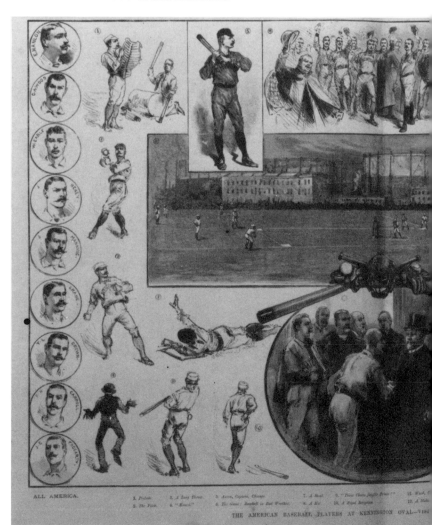

Two page spread showing the American Baseball Players at Kennington Oval—Visit of the Prince of Wales. Part of Spalding's All American Base Ball Tour of the world. From the *Illustrated London News* , April 6, 1889. *From the Kashmanian Collection.*

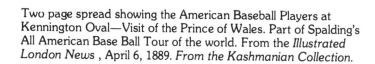

The Brooklyn Baseball Club of the outlaw Players League, coached by Monte Ward who is seated in the center of the middle row. The league lasted only one year. Copyrighted by G.W. Smith, 1890. 17" x 13". *From the Kashmanian Collection.*

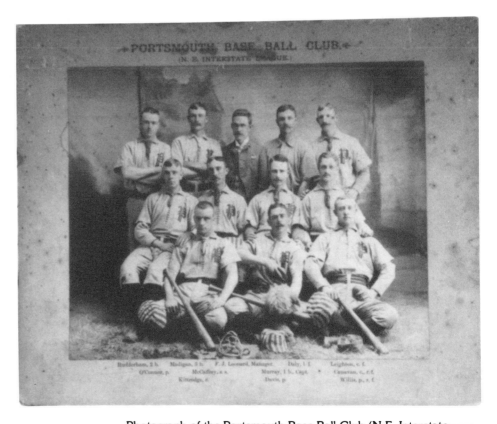

Photograph of the Portsmouth Base Ball Club (N.E. Interstate League). L.V. Newell & Co. photographers, Portsmouth, New Hampshire, c. 1890. The players: *top row* Rudderham, Madigan, F.J. Leonard, manager, Sun Daly (Baltimore, 1892), John Leighton (Syracuse National, 1890); *middle row* Frank O'Connor (Philadelphia, 1893), McCaffrey, Murray, Canavan; *bottom row* Mal Kittredge (Chicago 1890-1897, active in the majors to 1906), George Davis (Cleveland, 1891), Willis. 12" x 10". *From the Kashmanian Collection.*

Fat Man's Base Ball team, c. 1890. L.V. Newell & Co. Portrait and landscape photographers, Portsmouth, New Hampshire. *From the Kashmanian Collection.*

Menu and program for a dinner presented to honor the Cincinnati Reds, National League and World's Champions, 1919. September 27, 1919, Hotel Gibson, Cincinnati. 8.75″ long. *From the Kashmanian Collection.*

The 1908 Championship Tigers, C.M.H. Ames and Co., Detroit. *Courtesy of Mike Brown.*

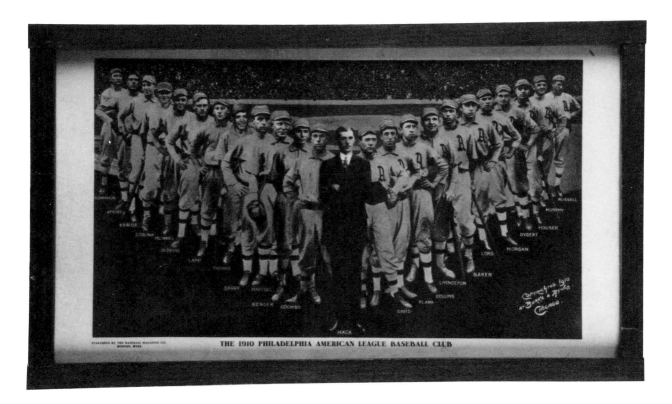

Philadelphia Athletics 1910. Published by the Baseball Magazine Co., Boston, Mass. The players: Francis (?) Donahue, Tommy Atkins, Harry Krause, Amos Strunk, Stuffy McInnes (sic), Rube Oldring, Jack Lapp, Ira Thomas, Jack Barry, Topsy Hartsel, Chief Bender, Jack Coombs, Connie Mack, Harry Davis, Eddie Plank, Eddie Collins, Paddy Livingston, Frank "Home Run" Baker, Bris Lord, Cy Morgan, Jimmy Dygert, Ben Houser, Danny Murphy, Russell. Copyrighted 1910 by Burke & Atwell, Chicago. 20" x 11.5". *From the Kashmanian Collection.*

The All Star Masonic Game photograph features major league players who belonged to the Masonic Organization. Trenton, New Jersey, 1935. Bottom row, left to right: Tiny Parker, umpire, Sam Jones, Lefty Grove, Sam Foxx, Jimmy Foxx, Rip Collins, Cliff Case from the masons, Max Bishop, Herb Pennock, Charles Gilbert, Frankie Hayes; middle row: Hulet, Ethan Allen, George Davis, Dazzy Vance, Waite Hoyt, Red Rolfe, Curley Ogden, Dick Porter; Top row: Charley Hargreaves, George Earnshaw, Bucky Walters, Rube Walburg, Jim Pattison, Lena Blackburn. Photo by Moyer. *Courtesy of Ted Patterson.*

Team Photo of the champion Newark Bears minor league club, c. 1932. Among those on the team Johnny Murphy, Dixie Walker, Red Rolfe, Johnny Neun & others made major leagues in future years. *Courtesy of Ted Patterson.*

Autographed photo of the Brooklyn Dodgers, National League Champions, 1952. By Verna Photographers, Brooklyn, New York. 48.5″ x 10″. *From the Kashmanian Collection.*

# The Negro Leagues and African-American Baseball

Trade card for Page Woven Wire Fence Company, Adrian, Michigan, featuring the "Page Fence Giants" base ball club. c. 1895. The players: *standing* , Charles Grant, Joe Miller, George Wilson, Grant Johnson, John Patterson; *seated* , William Binga, Pete Burns, A.S. Parsons, manager, Ed Woods, Billy Holland, George Taylor. *From the Kashmanian Collection.*

Front view of the fence company trade card.

Trade card for Page Woven Wire Fence Company, Adrian, Michigan, featuring the "Page Fence Giants" Base Ball Club. The players: *back row* , George Taylor, George Wilson, Grant Johnson, Joe Miller; *middle row* , "Billy" Holland, A.S. Parsons, manager, Pete Burns; *front row* , Fred Van Dyke, William Binga, Charles Grant, Vasco Graham. 4.5″ x 3.5″. *From the Kashmanian Collection.*

Old photograph of an African-American baseball team taken circa
1907, in Morgantown, West Virginia. The players: *top row* ,
Johnson, Crawford, Jenkins, Parker, Brooks, Jenkins, Ward;
*bottom row* , Ben Smith, Snow Parker, Hosby, Bakey, Ogden,
Coffee Henderson. Overall size 8″ x 10″. *From the Kashmanian
Collection.*

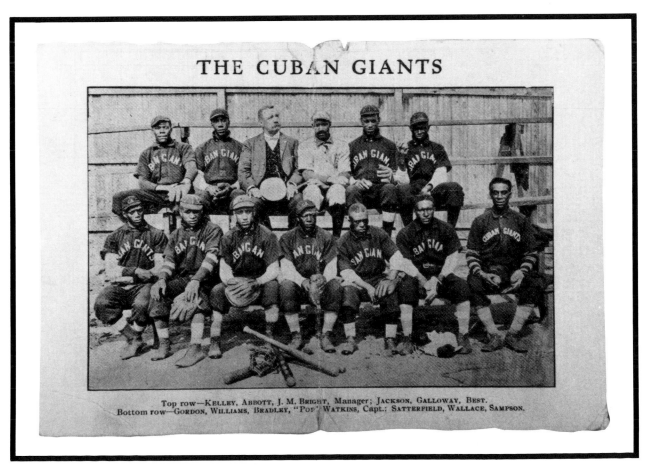

The Cuban Giants score card, c. 1900-1910. The players: *top row* ,
Kelley, Abbott, J.M. Bright, manager, Jackson, Galloway, Bent;
*bottom row* , Gordon, Williams, Bradley, "Pop" Watkins, Captain,
Satterfield, Wallace, Sampson. 8″ x 5.5″. *From the Kashmanian
Collection.*

Post card for the Philadelphia Black Giants, circa 1908. The players: *top row* , Addison, Pierce, Barber, Waide, Fisher; *middle row* , -?-, Thomas, H.W. Schuchter, owner, Poles, McClellan, captain; *bottom row* , Francis, James. 3.5″ x 5.5″. *From the Kashmanian Collection.*

Postcard of Peter's Union Giants, Chicago, c. 1910. 3.5″ x 5.5″. *From the Kashmanian Collection.*

"When the Cuban Giants Came to Livonia," circa 1910. 3.5″ x 5.5″. *From the Kashmanian Collection.*

Remaining portion of a photo postcard of the Buffalo Giants baseball team in 1910. *From the Kashmanian Collection.*

# BASE BALL.

## HOWARD HILLS
### VS
### Blackstone Colored Giants, of Prov.
### Sunday, June 2nd, 1912.

TICKETS - - - - 15 CENTS

Base ball ticket to see Howard Hills play the Blackstone Colored Giants of Providence, Rhode Island, Sunday, June 2, 1912. 3.75" x 1/75". *From the Kashmanian Collection.*

Pre-game snapshot of representatives of the Breakers Hotel and the Royal Poinciana Hotel, Palm Beach, Florida, c. 1917. During the winter, the hotels hired African-American baseball players to play games for the entertainment of the guests. Photographed by Edward F. Foley. 3.5" x 5.75". *From the Kashmanian Collection.*

The Hilldale Youth Base Ball Team, Darby, Pennsylvania, c. 1915. In the 1920s they would evolve into the powerful Philadelphia Hilldale Base Ball Club of the Negro Leagues. Photo size: 6" x 8". *From the Kashmanian Collection.*

The Detroit Stars baseball team, 1921. Photograph, 13.5" x 5.5". *From the Kashmanian Collection.*

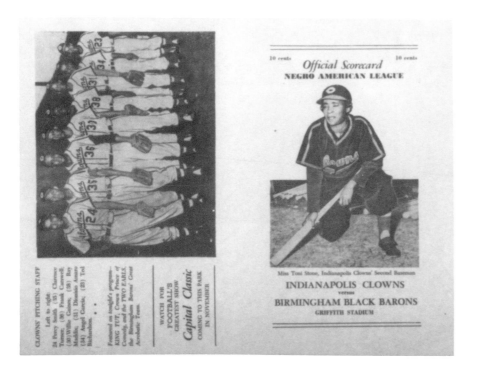

1953 Negro American League scorecard with photo of woman player, Miss Toni Stone, Indianapolis Clowns' second baseman. Clowns versus the Birmingham Black Barons, Griffith Stadium, Washington, D.C. The players on the left: *left to right* : Percy Smith, Clarence Turner, Frank Carswell, Willy Gaines, Ray Maddix, Dionisio Amaro, Angel Garcia, Ted Richardson. With the integration of base ball, the Negro Leagues lost most of their talent. Of these players only Frank Carswell spent time in the majors, playing with Detroit in 1953. 8.5″ x 11″ unfolded. *From the Kashmanian Collection.*

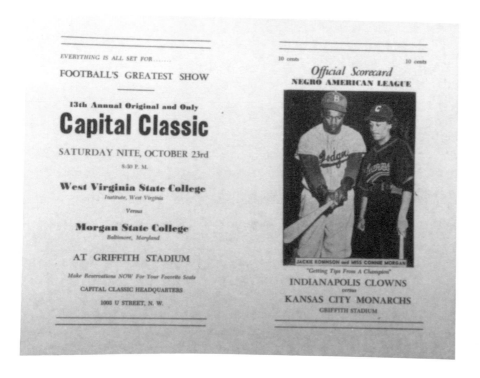

Trophy for the Camel Stars of the R.J. Reynolds Tobacco Co. League, "Colored Winners" of the 1921 season. 9.5″ x 7″. *Courtesy of Thomas Gray.*

1954 Negro American League scorecard featuring Jackie Robinson and Miss Connie Morgan. Indianapolis Clowns versus the Kansas City Monarchs, Griffith Stadium, Washington, D.C. *From the Kashmanian Collection.*

# Team Postcards

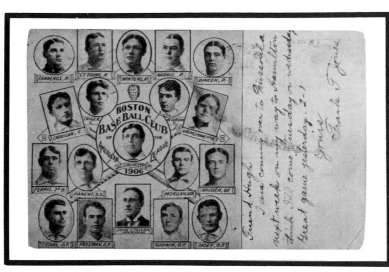

The championship New York National Baseball Team of 1904. In the center is John McGraw, the manager. Photos by Carl Y. Horner, Boston. Card by Rotograph Co., New York. 3.25" x 5.25". *From the Kashmanian Collection.*

Boston Base Ball Club of the American League, 1906. The players: *top row* Jesse Tannehill, Cy Young, George Winters, Joe Harris, Bill Dinneen; *2nd row* Bill Carrigan, Lou Criger, Bob Peterson, Moose Grimshaw; *3rd row* Hobe Ferris, Freddy Parent, James J. Collins, manager and third base, Red Morgan, Jack Hayden, Chick Stahl, Buck Freeman, John Taylor, President, Goodwin, John Hoey. Sporting Life Publishing Co., Philadelphia, Pennsylvania. 3.5" x 5.5". *From the Kashmanian Collection.*

The Cubs, Chicago National League Ball Club, 1906 pennant winners. The players: *top row* Three Finger Brown, Jack Pfeister, Solly Hofman, C.G. Williams, Orval Overall, Ed Reulbach, Johnny Kling; *middle row*, Doc Gessler, Jack Taylor, Harry Steinfeldt, J. McCormick, Frank Chance, Jimmy Sheckard, Pat Moran, Frank "Wildfire" Schulte; *bottom row*, Carl Lundgren, Tom Walsh, Johnny Evers, Jimmy Slagle, Joe Tinker. Post card published by V.O. Hammon Publishing Co., Chicago. *From the Kashmanian Collection.*

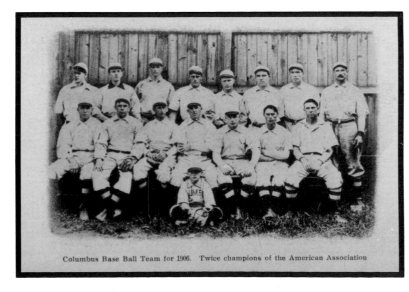

The Columbus Base Ball Team of 1906, twice champions of the American Association. One of a series of *Columbus Dispatch* post cards which consisted of 16 subjects. 3.625" x 5.5". *From the Kashmanian Collection.*

The 1906 pennant winning Detroit Tigers. Copyrighted by Heimer. The players: *top row* , John Eubanks, Claude Rossman, Sam Crawford, Wild Bill Donovan, George Mullin, Ed Willits (sic), Fred Payne, Ed Killian; *middle row,* Davy Jones, Red Downs, Ty Cobb, Bill Coughlin, Germany Schaefer, Elijah Jones; *bottom row,* Ed Seiver (sic), Jimmy Archer, Hughie Jennings, manager, Boss Schmidt, Charlie O'Leary; *reclining,* O'Brien, the mascot. 3.5" x 5.5". *From the Kashmanian Collection.*

The New Bedford team of the New England League, 1907. Vibbert, The Worcester Photo Co., Worcester, Massachusetts. 4" x 5.5". *From the Kashmanian Collection.*

The 1907 Brooklyn Baseball team. The players: *standing,* George G. Bell, Nap Rucker, John E. Hummell, Al Burch, Harry McIntire, Tim Jordan, Harry Lumley, Bill Bergen, Jim Pastorius, Elmer Stricklett; *seated,* Doc Scanlon, Billy Maloney, Whitey Alpermann, Lew Ritter, Patsy Donovan, H.W. Medicus, Phil Lewis, Doc Casey, and Emil Batch. Eagle Press, Brooklyn. 3.5" x 5.5". *From the Kashmanian Collection.*

Postcard for the New York Highlanders, 1911. The team's first president was Joseph Gordon, and name Highlanders comes from the famous British military regiment, the Gordon Highlanders. By the time of this photograph, however they were already being called the Yankees. The players: *from the top left* , Jack Quinn, Mike Fitzgerald, Hal Chase, manager, John Knight, Jeff Sweeney; *from elbow to elbow* , Lynch, Birdie Cree, Jack Warhop, Otis Johnson; *lower left hand corner* , Harry Wolter, Russ Ford, Johnnie Priest, Charlie Hemphill, Bert Daniels; *from the chest down,* Bob Williams, Farrell, Earl Gardner, Hippo Vaughn, Roy Hartzel (sic), Ray Fisher; *lower right hand corner* Roxy Roach, Ray Caldwell, Walter Blair. Copyright by the Sporty Postal Card Co., Newark, New Jersey. 3.5" x 5.5". *From the Kashmanian Collection.*

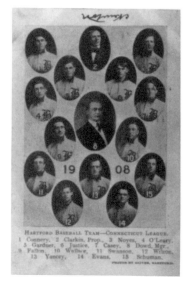

The Hartford Baseball Team of the Connecticut League, c. 1908. Photos by Oliver, Hartford. Published by A.W. Spargo, Hartford. *From the Kashmanian Collection.*

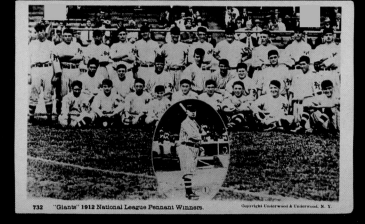

732  "Giants" 1912 National League Pennant Winners.     Copyright Underwood & Underwood, N. Y.

The 1912 National League pennant winning Giants. Underwood & Underwood, New York. 3.5" x 5.5". *From the Kashmanian Collection.*

742  1912 American League Pennant Winners.     Copyright Underwood & Underwood, N. Y.

The 1912 Red Sox, American League Champions. Underwood and Underwood, New York. 3.5" x 5.5". *From the Kashmanian Collection.*

SEASON 1912
CHAMPIONS OF THE AMERICAN LEAGUE
BOSTON RED SOX

Another postcard of the 1912 Red Sox. The players are named on their chests. The Photo Art Shop, Swampscott, Massachusetts. 3.5" x 5.5". *From the Kashmanian Collection.*

Team photo for the Red Sox, c. 1912. The back has space to report the results of games between Boston and New York. The players (left to right): Steve Yerkes, Smokey Joe Wood, Hugh Bedient, Les Nunamaker, Harry Hooper, Chick Stahl, Bill Carrigan, Heinie Wagner, Tris Speaker, Larry Pape, Marty Krug, Hick Cady, Clyde Engle, Olaf Henriksen, Charlie Hall, Buck O'Brien, Hugh Bradley, Duffy Lewis. Copyright Technical Book Publishing Co. 3.5" x 7.25". *From the Kashmanian Collection.*

RED SOX — Left to Right : Yerkes, Wood Bedient, Nunamaker. Hooper, Stahl, Carrigan. Wagner, Speaker, Pape, Krug, Cady, Engle, Hendrickson, Hall, O'Brien, Bradley, Lewis.

The 1912 Cincinnati Red Legs, April, 1912. The players: *top row*, Hank Severeid, Tex McDonald, Bert Humphries, Art Fromme, Armando Marsans, Jim Bagby, Bob Keefe, Bill Prough, Harry Gasper (sic); *2nd row*, Rafael Almeide (sic), George Suggs, Miller, Williams, Larry McLean, Eddie Grant, Hanson Horsey, Mike Mitchell, Pietz; *3rd row, seated*, Tommy Clark (sic), Frank Smith, Rube Benton, Hank O'Day, manager, Dick Egan, Dick Hoblitzell, Bob Besher (sic), Johnny Bates; *front row*, Art Phelan, mascot Brownie Burke, Jimmy Esmond. Cincinnati ended the season in third place. F. Boellinger, Cincinnati, photographer and publisher. 3.5″ x 5.5″. *From the Kashmanian Collection.*

Postcard featuring the Boston Braves, Champions of 1914-1915. The players: *top row*, Bill James, Ted Cather, Charlie Deal, George Davis, Ensign Cottrell, Otto Hess, Les Mann, Hank Gowdy, Butch Schmidt, Bert Whaling; *middle row*, Possum Whitted, Oscar Dugey, Fred Tyler, Paul Strand, Josh Devore, Red Smith, Larry Gilbert, Herbie Moran (mistakenly identified as P.J. Moran); *bottom row*, Joe Connolly, Fred(?) Mitchell, coach, Willie Connor, mascot, Dick Rudolph, Rabbit Maranville, Dick Crutcher, Jack Martin, Johnny Evers. 4″ x 6″. *From the Kashmanian Collection.*

Olson's Cherokee Indian Base Ball Team, Watervliet, Michigan. Cross Photo. 3.375″ x 5.5″. *From the Kashmanian Collection.*

Color card for Green's Nebraska Indians. The card reads: "Established 1897. Only one on earth. Green's Nebraska Indian Baseball Team. Guy W. Green, Lincoln, Nebraska. Sole Owner and Manager. Lithographed in Germany. 3.5″ X 5.5″. *From the Kashmanian Collection.*

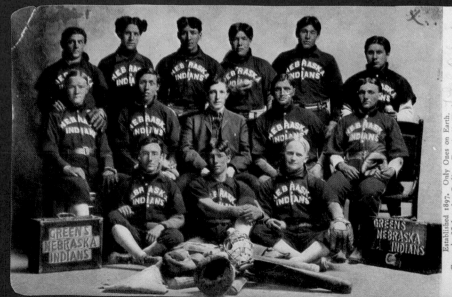

The 1935 American League champions, Detroit Tigers. The players: *front row* , Pete Fox, Jo-Jo White, Cy Perkins, Manager Mickey Cochrane, Del Baker, Flea Clifton, Goose Goslin; *2nd row,* Charlie Gehringer, Hugh Shelley, Marvin Owen, Ray Hayworth, Schoolboy Rowe, Elden Auker, Hank Greenberg; *3rd row* , Heinie Schuble, Vic Sorrell, Frank Reiber, Joe Sullivan, General Alvin Crowler, Gerry Walker; *back row* , Denny Carroll, trainer, Billy Rogell, Chief Hogsett, Tommy Bridges. 3.375" x 5.5". *From the Kashmanian Collection.*

"Greetings from the Giants," featuring Frank Bowerman, Red Ames, Sam Mertes, Christy Mathewson, Joe McGinnity, and Dummy Taylor. Copyright J.T. Dye, 1905. Published by Souvenir Post Card Co., New York. 3.5" x 5.5". *From the Kashmanian Collection.*

Color post card featuring the opening flag ceremony at Detroit stadium, c. 1907. 3.5" x 5.5". *From the Kashmanian Collection.*

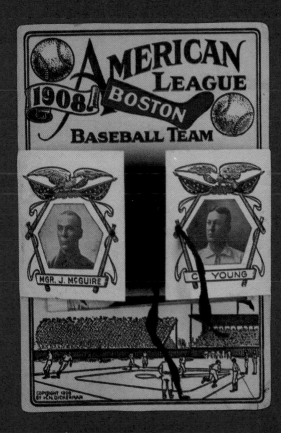

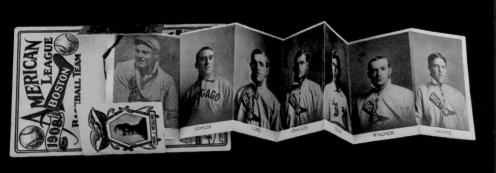

Postcard for the Boston American League Baseball Team, 1908. The pull-out, at left, has team photos. Copyright by H.N. Dickerman. *From the Kashmanian Collection.*

Boston Americans Red Sox post card. Beneath the baseball there is a pull-out section with players' photographs. Copyright 1908 by J.F. Furlong, Boston. 5.5″ x 3.5″. *From the Kashmanian Collection.*

**Opposite page:**
**Top right:**
Postcard of Washington Park, Brooklyn, c. 1910. Copyright, The Pictorial News Co., New York. 3.5″ x 5.5″. *From the Kashmanian Collection.*

**Center Left:**
The American League Base Ball Park, New York. Thaddeus Wilkerson, New York. 3.5″ x 5.5″. *From the Kashmanian Collection.*

**Bottom Right:**
American League Base Ball Park, New York, New York, c. 1910. 3.5″ x 5.5″. *From the Kashmanian Collection.*

Postcard of the Detroit Tigers with fold-out of the team, 1908. Art Post Card Co., Publishers, Detroit, Michigan. *From the Kashmanian Collection.*

Hoegee Baseball Club, Los Angeles, c. 1910-1915. Hoegee was a manufacturer of sporting goods at 136 South Main, Los Angeles. 3.5″ x 5.5″. *From the Kashmanian Collection.*

**Fields of Battle**
Postcards

Brooklyn Base Ball Park, 1909.

American League Base Ball Park, New York.

American League Base Ball Park, New York, N.Y.

25893

"Home of the Reds, Palace of the Fans," c. 1910. Postcard published by S.H. Knox & Co. *From the Kashmanian Collection.*

The National League Ball Park, Cincinnati, Ohio. The Norwood Souvenir Co., Cincinnati, Ohio, 1911. Postcard, 3.5″ x 5.5″. *From the Kashmanian Collection.*

The Ball Park at Cleveland, c. 1916. The Braun Post Card Co., Cleveland. 3.5″ x 5.5″. *From the Kashmanian Collection.*

Fenway Park, Boston, Massachusetts. Published by A. Israelson and Co., Roxbury, Massachusetts. Postcard, 3.5″ x 5.5″. *From the Kashmanian Collection.*

The Polo Grounds, New York. Thaddeus Wilkerson, New York. 3.5″ x 5.5″. *From the Kashmanian Collection.*

Another view of the Polo Grounds, New York. Thaddeus Wilkerson, New York. 3.5″ x 5.5″. *From the Kashmanian Collection.*

Color postcard of the interior of Forbes Field, Pittsburgh, Pennsylvania, c. 1909. Chatauqua Photographic Co., Pittsburgh, Pennsylvania. 3.5″ x 11″. *From the Kashmanian Collection.*

152:—Exterior Shibe Baseball Stadium, Philadelphia, Pa.

Postcard of the exterior of Shibe Baseball Stadium, Philadelphia, Pennsylvania, c. 1915. Published by P. Sander, Philadelphia and Atlantic City. *From the Kashmanian Collection.*

"Nuf Ced," McGreavey's Boston bar and personal collection of sports memorabilia. McGreavey was involved in the Royal Rooters, a Red Sox fan club. The bar which once stood at Columbia Avenue and Whittier Street burned to the ground, but some of the collection survives at the Boston Public Library. Circa 1906. 3.5″ x 5.5″. *From the Kashmanian Collection.*

Shibe Park Baseball Ground, Philadelphia, Pa.

Shibe Park Baseball Ground, Philadelphia, Pennsylvania. Postcard, 3.375″ x 5.375″. *From the Kashmanian Collection.*

# Awards

Loving cup trophy presented to Dick Rudolph of the 1914 World Champion Boston Braves. It was given to him by his Bronx friends and admirers for winning three games in the World Series. 22" x 11" diameter. *From the Kashmanian Collection.*

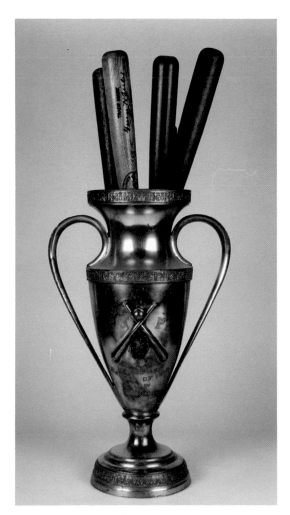

Trophy from Fisk Poli Trophy Series, 1915. 19". *Courtesy of Mike Brown.*

Bat presented to the Pioneer Base Ball Club of West Quincy, Massachusetts, championship club of Quincy and Braintree for the season of 1876. The wood is laminated walnut and maple, by F.A. Spear. 37". *From the Kashmanian Collection.*

"The Pitcher" trophy given by Spalding to various industrial teams. This was presented to the Tulsa Oil League's Cosden & Company team. 19.5″ x 8″. Dieges & Clust, c. 1922. *Courtesy of Mike Brown.*

"The Catcher" trophy. 18″ x 8″. *Courtesy of Mike Brown.*

Presentation gift given by Ban Johnson, President of the American League, to the Government of Mexico for the encouragement and expansion of the game through our "sister nation." Given through the president of Mexico, Alvaro Obregon, 1923. 5.5″. *From the Kashmanian Collection.*

Trophy to D.J. Klinedinst, President, C.Y.C.L., 1934, silver and cast iron. 4″ x 2.25″. *Courtesy of Mike Brown.*

Charm for the 1955 world's champion Brooklyn Dodgers. Dieges & Clust, 14k gold. 1.5″ x 1.125″. *From the Kashmanian Collection.*

# Chapter 4
# *Tools of the Game*

In the earliest days of the game, equipment needs were minimal. A ball, a stick, and four sticks or bags to serve as bases. The fielders played barehanded, capturing the ball with both hands pivoting at the heals like a clam shell. The catcher stood well behind the batter, hoping to get the ball on the bounce.

The batter used a long, straight bat, radically different from the cricket bat, and lacking the shapeliness and balance of later bats. Generally the bat was as long as the batter could comfortably handle, giving great leverage.

The large balls were homemade or wool and rubber tightly wrapped. They had a great deal of bounce, often going over the fielder's head. Indeed, catching the ball on the bounce was once considered an out. They were pitched underhanded. In the early 1870s A.G. Spalding lobbied for a uniform ball to be used throughout the game. This would help limit some of the excessively high scores of early baseball, while at the same time earning Spalding a royalty on each ball manufactured. Henry Chadwick described the regulation ball in *DeWitt's Base Ball Guide* of 1876: "The ball must weigh not less than 5 nor more than 5¼ ounces avoirdupois. It must measure not less than 9 nor more than 9¼ inches in circumference. It must be

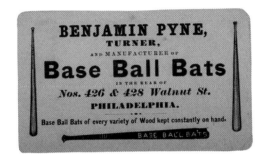

1870s business card for Benjamin Pyne, base ball bat maker. *From the Kashmanian Collection.*

## Advertising and Catalogues for Equipment

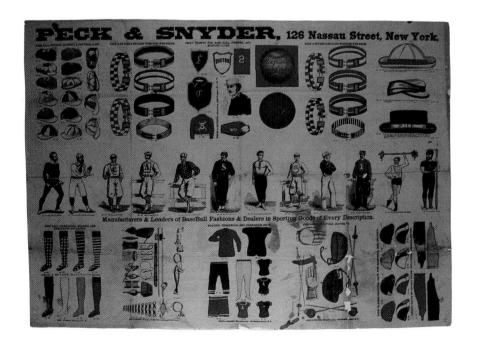

Peck & Snyder of New York was one of the earliest companies specializing in sporting goods. This broadside shows some of the products offered by the largest equipment supplier of the time, c. 1870s. Note the variety of fashions used in the early days of baseball. 26.5" x 36.25". *From the Kashmanian Collection.*

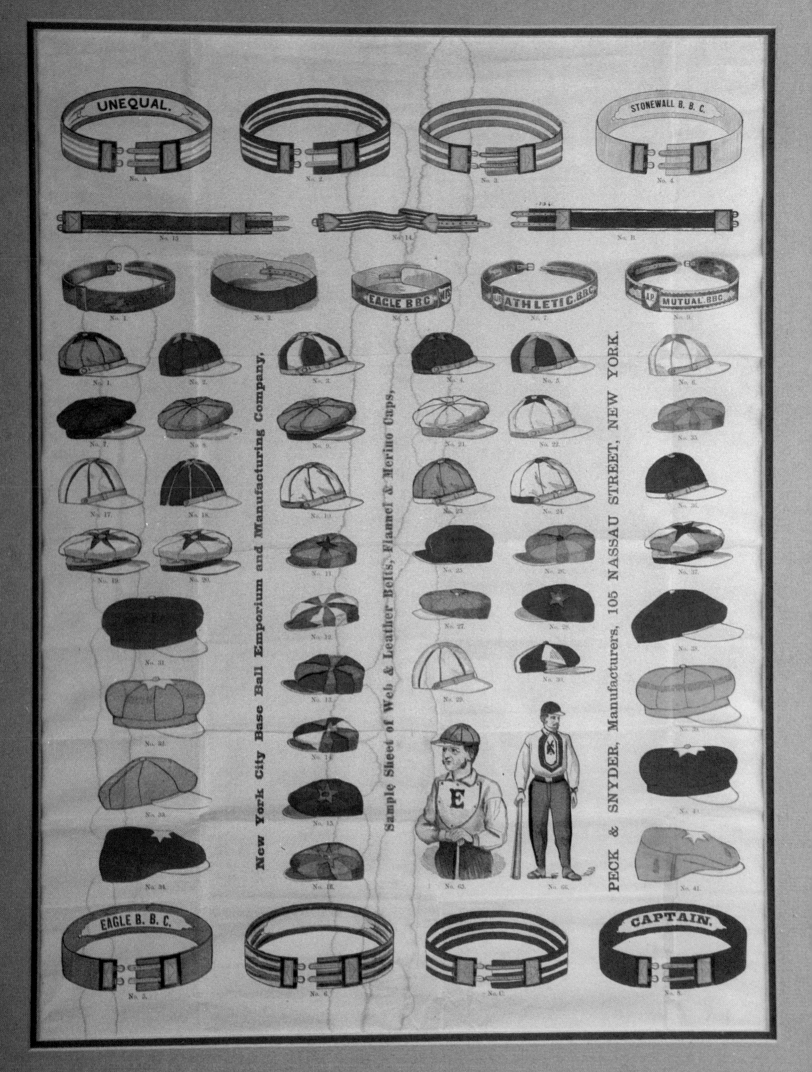

composed of woolen yarn and shall not contain more than one ounce of vulcanized rubber in mold form and shall be covered with leather and furnished by the secretary of the league." (quoted in *Baseball and the American Dream*, page 35.)

Catchers were the first to use added equipment. The mask was developed by a Harvard baseball player named F. Webster Thayer, and took some years to overcome its "sissy" image. Catchers also were the first to use padded gloves, and in the nineties added shin guards and chest protectors.

Other players started wearing thin leather gloves which may have taken away a bit of the sting, but did little to improve performance. Smith reports that second baseman Arthur Irvin was the first fielder to use a padded glove to protect a broken finger. When he was not booed from the field, other players began to wear padded gloves too.

Uniforms were gaily colored and nearly identical to the firefighters uniforms of the day. The bib on the chest carried the letter of the team, as did the brass belt buckle. The shoes were high-topped leather with cricket spikes, either built-in or attached at the time of the game.

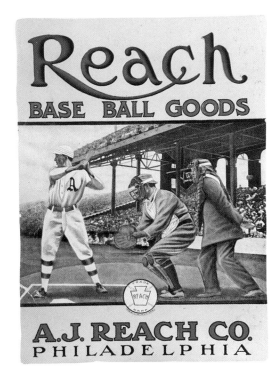

Reach Base Ball Goods catalog, 1912, with Philadelphia team batter on cover. A.J. Reach Co., Philadelphia. 5″ x 7″. *From the Kashmanian Collection.*

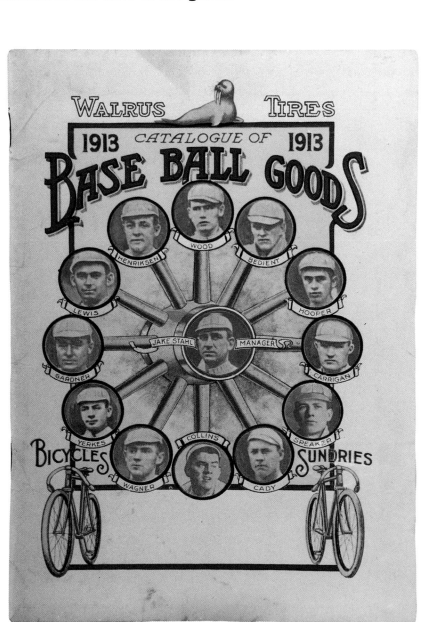

**Opposite page:**
Hand-colored advertising broadside for baseball equipment from Peck and Snyder Base Ball Emporium and Manufacturing Company, New York City. c. 1870s. 16″ x 22″. *From the Kashmanian Collection.*

Walrus Tires Catalogue of Base Ball Goods, 1913. It features the champion 1912 Boston Red Sox of the American League. The players *clockwise from the top center* : Smokey Wood, Hugh Bedient, Harry Hooper, Bill Carrigan, Tris Speaker, Hick Cady, Bill (?) Collins, Heinie Wagner, Steve Yerkes, Larry Gardner, Duffy Lewis, Olaf Henriksen; *center* , Jake Stahl, Manager. 5.5″ x 7.5″. *From the Kashmanian Collection.*

Hanging sign for Reach Base Ball Goods. WNW, artist's initials. Al Reach was among the pioneers of professional baseball, playing for the Philadelphia Athletics in the National Association from 1871-1875. He returned to coach in Philadelphia in 1890, long after he had established a successful sports equipment company. 16" x 12". *Courtesy of Ted Patterson.*

Reach Baseball Goods hanging sign, A.J. Reach Co., Toronto and Philadelphia. W.N.W., artist's initials. 15.75" x 11.5". *Courtesy of Ted Patterson.*

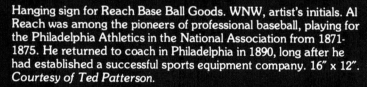

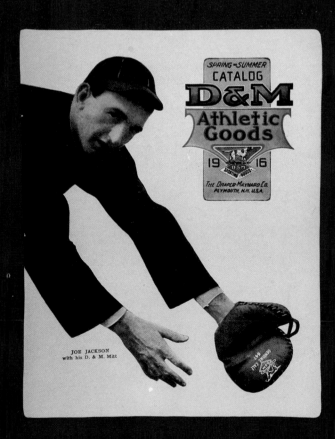

Business card from the Honus Wagner Sporting Goods Company, Pittsburgh, Pennsylvania. Honus Wagner was president of the company. 2.625" x 4.625". *From the Kashmanian Collection.*

A 1916 Draper & Maynard, Plymouth, New Hampshire, athletic goods catalog with "Shoeless" Joe Jackson on cover. *From the Kashmanian Collection.*

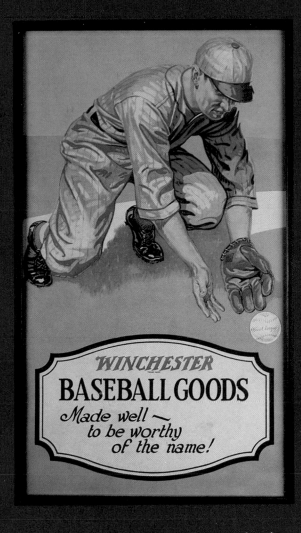

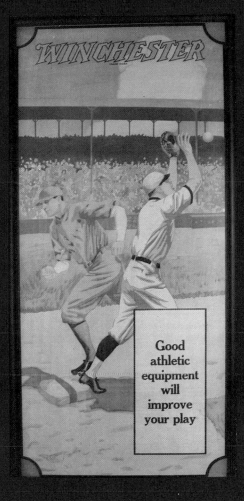

Winchester Baseball Goods sign. Winchester produced a general line of sporting goods and was most well-known for its firearms line. The ball is imprinted with "Official League." Paper, 31" x 17". *Courtesy of Ted Patterson.*

Winchester Baseball Goods sign. Paper, 36" x 16.5". *Courtesy of Ted Patterson.*

A.G. Spalding & Bros. advertisement for the Frank Frisch model glove, 1927. The company was founded in 1876. Another of the early baseball players who went into the manufacturing business, Al Spalding played for the Boston Red Stockings in the National Association from 1871-1875. He moved to Chicago where he played in the National League from 1876-1878 as player coach and started his sporting goods business. 13.5" x 21.5". *Courtesy of Ted Patterson.*

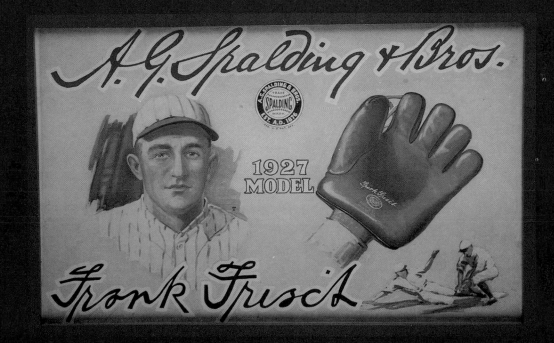

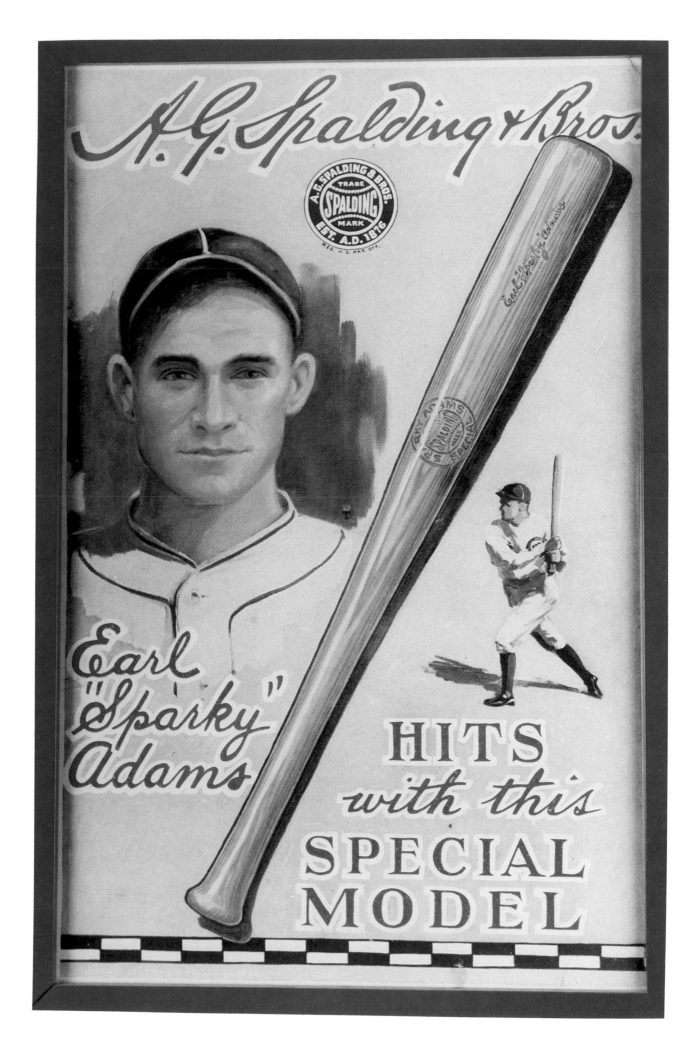

A.G. Spalding & Bros. advertisement featuring the Sparkey Adams bat. Paper, 13.5" x 21.5". *Courtesy of Ted Patterson.*

A.G. Spalding & Bros. advertisement for baseball gloves featuring the Stanley Harris model glove, 1927. 13.5″ x 21.5″. *Courtesy of Ted Patterson.*

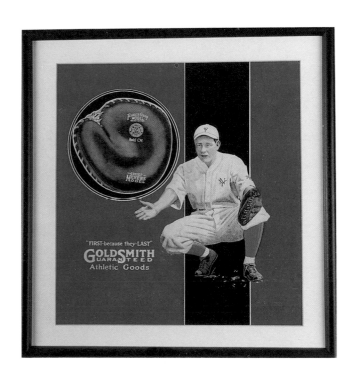

Hanging sign for Goldsmith Athletic Goods with Chief Meyers. Cardboard, 12.75″ x 14″. *Courtesy of Ted Patterson.*

Advertising poster with Ted Williams for Hillerich & Bradsby Co., Inc., Louisville, Kentucky, 1947. Sam Davis, artist. 15″ x 20″. *From the Kashmanian Collection.*

Mickey Vernon in this advertising poster for Hillerich & Bradsby Co. Sam Davis, artist. Autographed by Mickey Vernon. 18.5″ x 13.75″. *Courtesy of Ted Patterson.*

Die-cut Wilson advertisement with Al Kaline's photograph and facsimile signature. 7″ x 6″. *From the Kashmanian Collection.*

"World's Famous Base Ball Players" advertisement from Goldsmith Sporting Goods. Clockwise from the top right, the players are Johnny Evers, Hans Wagner, Walter Johnson, Ty Cobb, Edward Collins, Napoleon LaJoie, Frank Chance, Christy Mathewson, Johnny Kling, and Jimmy Sheckard. Paper foldout, 12″ x 19″. *Courtesy of Ted Patterson.*

# Bats

1860s bat, W.A. Marshall, Ajax Base Ball Club. 37.5". *From the Kashmanian Collection.*

Spalding Mushroom bat from the late-1890s to early-1900s. *From the Congdon-Martin Collection.*

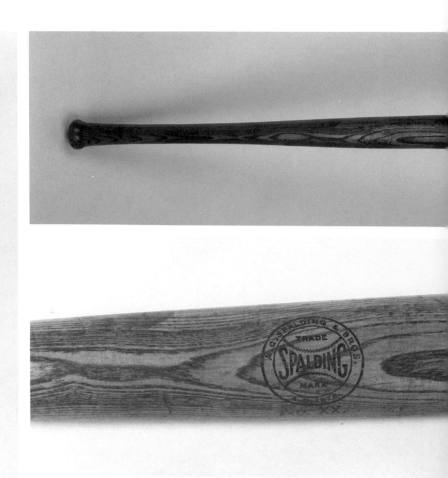

A.G. Spalding & Bros. No. XX, with nice baseball logo, c. 1900-1910. 33.75″. *From the Kashmanian Collection.*

Victor Sporting Goods Co., No. 101, c. 1900. Painted logo. *From the Kashmanian Collection.*

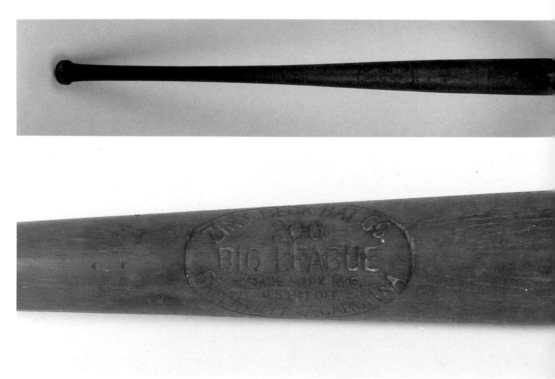

Zinn Beck Bat Co. Greenville, S. Carolina, No. 200, "Big League." 36″. *From the Kashmanian Collection.*

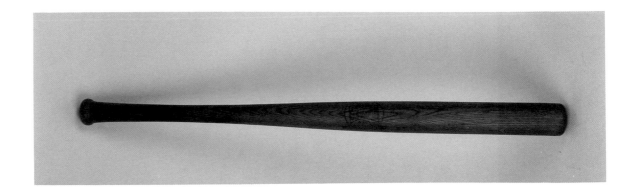

Goldsmith, No. 38. 34″. *From the Kashmanian Collection.*

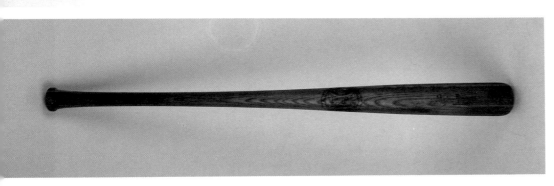

Spalding No. 189 with a nice baseball logo. "Major League" model. 34″ *From the Kashmanian Collection.*

Lajoie bats. On the bottom is a Wright & Ditson bat, Boston, Pat. Dec. 29, 1903. The Wright of "Wright & Ditson" was George Wright, pioneer player on the Red Stockings of Cincinnati and Boston professional teams, and brother of Harry Wright. Like Reach and Spalding he went into the sports equipment business and was later bought out by Spalding. On the top is double handle bat of the style used by Lajoie. Both marked Lajoie and measuring 33.5″. *From the Kashmanian Collection.*

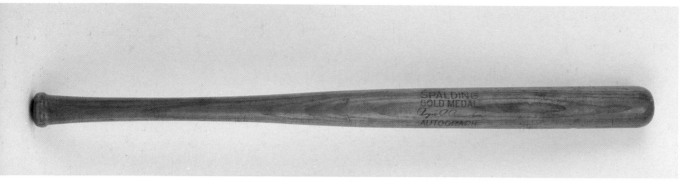

Spalding Gold Medal bat, c. 1910-1915, with facsimile autograph of
Roger P. Bresnahan. 32". *From the Kashmanian Collection.*

Wright & Ditson bat, Assorted Models, No. 150. Marked Walker.
34". *From the Kashmanian Collection.*

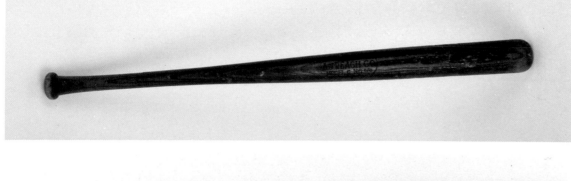

A.J. Reach & Co., "The Burley" model bat. 34". *From the
Kashmanian Collection.*

Stall & Dean, Tris Speaker bat with remains of a decal featuring Speaker's image. *From the Kashmanian Collection.*

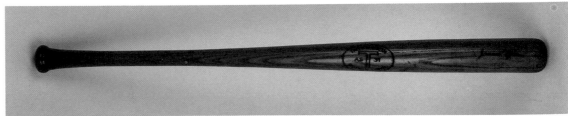

Tatem & Son, Putnam, Connecticut, AS 31, Jimmie Dykes model. 36″. *From the Kashmanian Collection.*

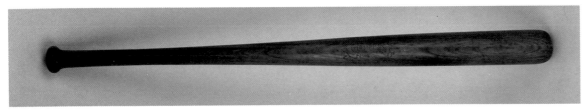

J.F Hillerich & Son, Louisville, "Champion, No. 7". Length: 35″. *From the Kashmanian Collection.*

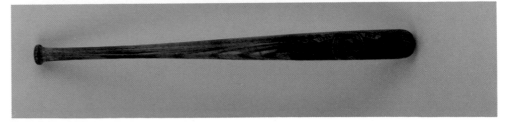

Miniature Louisville Slugger endorsed by E.T. Collins with portrait decal and signature. 14″. *From the Kashmanian Collection.*

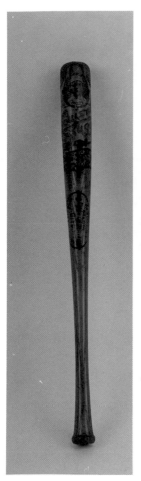

Miniature Louisville Slugger with a picture of Harry Davis, Philadelphia. Marked Hillerich & Sons in the decal and Hillerich & Bradsby on the brand. 14″. *From the Kashmanian Collection.*

Hillerich & Bradsby Co., Louisville Slugger, Georgia Peach bat with facsimile signature of Ty Cobb and his picture. 33.5″. *From the Kashmanian Collection.*

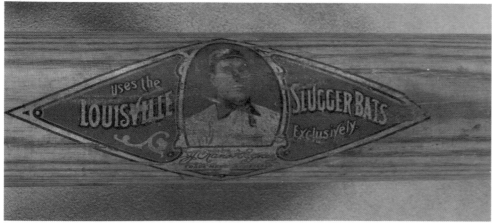

Louisville Slugger bat with portrait decal and facsimile signature of Honus Wagner by J.F. Hillerich & Son Co. Louisville, Kentucky. 31″. *From the Kashmanian Collection.*

Miniature Louisville Slugger bat with a decal picture of Ty Cobb, the Georgia Peach. Hillerich & Bradsby Co. 22″. *From the Kashmanian Collection.*

Hillerich & Bradsby, Louisville, Burnt Oil Finish, "Professional Model." 35.5″. *From the Kashmanian Collection.*

Hillerich & Bradsby, "King of the Field" No. 12. League Regulation. 33.75″. *From the Kashmanian Collection.*

Hillerich & Bradsby Co., Louisville Slugger, 40 C.K., Chuck Klein, "Bone Rubbed." Klein is in the Hall of Fame, 1980. 34″. *From the Kashmanian Collection.*

Hillerich & Bradsby Co., Louisville Slugger, 40 P.W., Paul Waner. Waner is a Hall of Famer. 35″. *From the Kashmanian Collection.*

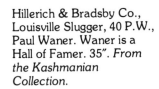

Hillerich & Bradsby, Louisville Slugger, 40 BRJ, George "Babe" Ruth, 32". *From the Kashmanian Collection.*

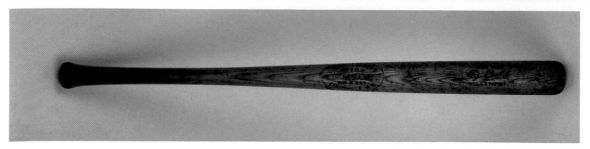

Hillerich & Bradsby, Louisville Slugger, 40 T.C.J. Ty Cobb model. 32". *From the Kashmanian Collection.*

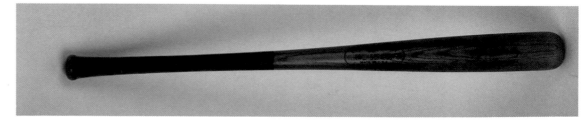

Hillerich & Bradsby Co., Louisville Slugger 40Z. "Jim Bottomley." Bottomley is a Hall of Famer. *From the Kashmanian Collection.*

Hillerich & Bradsby Co., Louisville Slugger, 40B.T. Wm. H. (Bill) Terry. Terry is a Hall of Famer. 33". *From the Kashmanian Collection.*

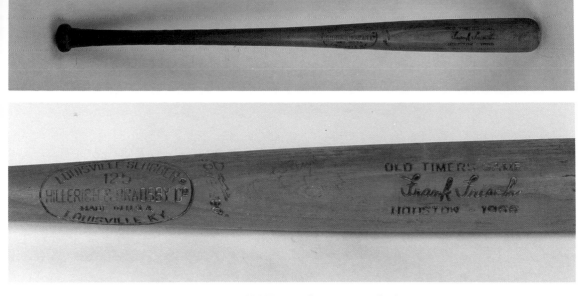

Bat used by Frank Frisch, Houston Old Timers Game, 1966. Code
F53 at the end of the bat. *From the Kashmanian Collection.*

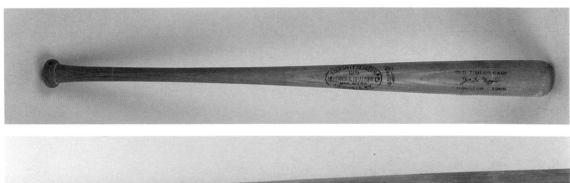

Hillerich & Bradsby Co., Louisville Slugger, 125. Bat used by Joe
DiMaggio in the Houston Old Timers Game, 1966. On the end of
the bat are numbers D29L indicating this was a bat actually used
by DiMaggio. 36". *From the Kashmanian Collection.*

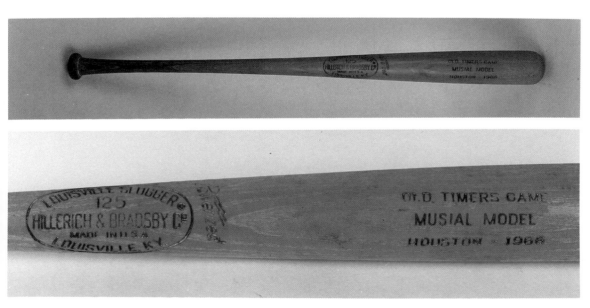

Bat used by Stan Musial, Houston Old Timers Game, 1966. Code
on the end is M 159. *From the Kashmanian Collection.*

## Balls and Gloves

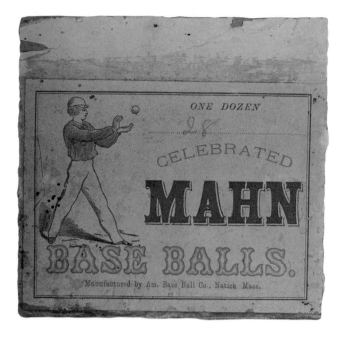

1870s label for Mahn Base Balls box, manufactured by the American Base Ball Company, Natick, Massachusetts. 5″ x 5″. *From the Kashmanian Collection.*

This baseball, probably from the 1880s, is three inches in diameter with a one piece covering and a weighted center. *Courtesy of Mike Brown.*

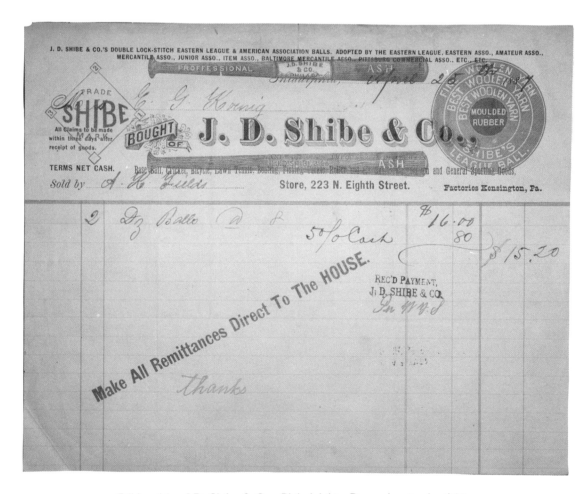

Bill head for J.D. Shibe & Co., Philadelphia, Pennsylvania, April 25, 1887. This family was very prominent in the history of the Philadelphia Athletics. At one time Ben Shibe was a horsecar driver who made baseballs on the side. The baseball business grew and eventually he came to own part of the Athletics. In 1909 he invested in the club again as it built a new stadium that was named in his honor. *From the Kashmanian Collection.*

Early soft toy baseball, 2.5″ in diameter, and an Al Simmons model glove for youth, c. 1920s. *Courtesy of Mike Brown.*

Official national league baseball, circa 1925, manufactured by Spalding, with original box. The glove on the left is a Paul Waner model glove, made by A. Reach Co. Inc., Philadelphia. The other is Dazzy Vance model glove, patented September 8, 1922, and made by Tryon, Philadelphia. *From the Kashmanian Collection.*

J. DeBeer and Son baseball, Albany, New York, c. 1930s.
*Courtesy of Mike Brown.*

Flexyde Baseball counter sign, for a ball manufactured by the
Goodyear Tire and Rubber Co., Akron, Ohio. A ball goes in hole
at the top. Kala Sign Co, Kalamazoo, Michigan, copyright 1926.
10.5" x 8.75". *Courtesy of Ted Patterson.*

Assorted baseball boxes. Notice the box on top from the Honus
Wagner Sporting Goods Co. *Courtesy of Mike Brown.*

DiMaggio baseball made in Japan in the 1930s. It was autographed in 1990. *Courtesy of Mike Brown.*

Pete Reiser model glove. MacGregor Goldsmith, c. 1940s. *From the Kashmanian Collection.*

Ted Williams glove, Sears, Roebuck & Co., made in Japan. *From the Kashmanian Collection.*

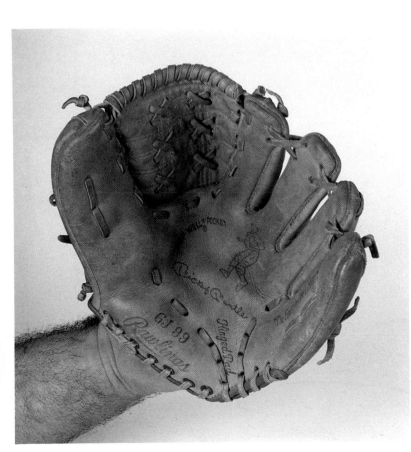

Rawlings Mickey Mantle model glove. *From the Kashmanian Collection.*

# Uniforms

Catcher's mask patented February 12, 1878. Manufacturer unknown. Steel and leather with cloth strap. The pad for the forehead pivots, while the chin pad is stationary. *From the Kashmanian Collection.*

Providence Gray's uniform worn by Albert "Bunny" Fabrique,
shortstop, 1914. Fabrique was a team mate of Babe Ruth on this
minor league club and went on to play for Brooklyn, 1916-1917.
*From the Kashmanian Collection.*

Clyde Barnhart's jersey from Pittsburgh Pirates, 1925. The rare patch signifies 50th anniversary of the league, 1876-1925. *Courtesy of Ted Patterson.*

Rocky Colavito's Cleveland Indians jersey and cap, from the 1958 home uniform. Autographed. *Courtesy of Ted Patterson.*

George Kell's 1949 Detroit cap. *Courtesy of Ted Patterson.*

The St. Louis Browns cap of Bobby Young, 1951. *Courtesy of Ted Patterson.*

Bob Feller's jersey, Cleveland Indians, 1958, #19. *Courtesy of Ted Patterson.*

Two Oriole caps, 1958 and 1963. The 1963 cap is part of the home uniform. *Courtesy of Ted Patterson.*

The Orioles cap of Boog Powell, 1966. *Courtesy of Ted Patterson.*

Dick Phillips's jersey, Washington Senators, autographed, 1963. *Courtesy of Ted Patterson.*

Steve Barber's jersey, Baltimore Orioles, 1965, autographed, and an Orioles cap (not his). The same style uniform was used by Baltimore from 1963-1965. *Courtesy of Ted Patterson.*

Ray Fossey's All-Star Game jersey, summer weight, Cleveland Indians, 1970. Autographed. *Courtesy of Ted Patterson.*

Dick Hall's jersey, Orioles, 1971. *Courtesy of Ted Patterson.*

Jim Bouton's jersey, Houston, 1970, autographed. *Courtesy of Ted Patterson.*

Jim Rice's rookie year jersey, Boston, 1974, autographed. *Courtesy of Ted Patterson.*

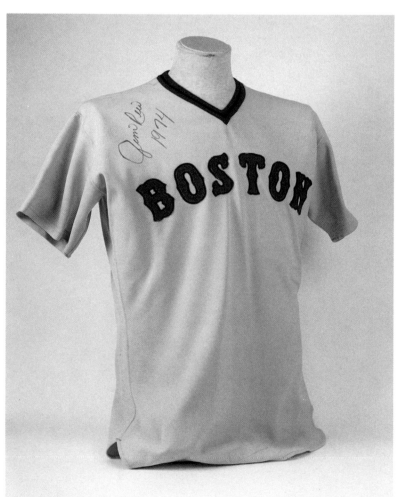

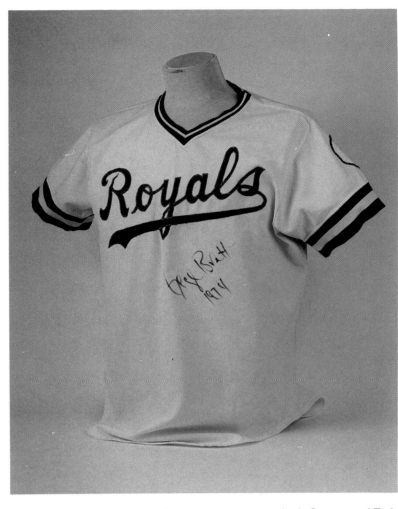

George Brett's jersey, Royals, 1974, autographed. *Courtesy of Ted Patterson.*

Mike Schmidt's jersey and cap, Philadelphia Phillies, 1981. *Courtesy of Ted Patterson.*

Steve Carlton's jersey, Philadelphia Phillies, 1975. *Courtesy of Ted Patterson.*

Rich "Goose" Gossage's jersey with cap, New York, 1979. *Courtesy of Ted Patterson.*

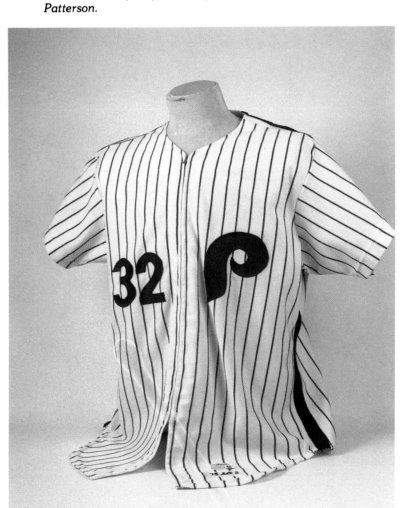

The last wool flannel jersey worn by Frank Robinson. This had been the jersey of Galliher, who never made the team, worn by Robinson for one season because Don Sutton would not give up the number 20. 1972. Autographed. *Courtesy of Ted Patterson.*

A Boston Red Sox jersey, cap, and bat that belonged to Carl Yastrzemski, 1983. The jersey is autographed. *Courtesy of Ted Patterson.*

Baseball caps: Don Sutton, California, 1986; Gaylord Perry, San Diego, late 1970s, signed; Vita Blue, Oakland A's, numbered 35. *Courtesy of Ted Patterson.*

Rusty Staub's jersey, Mets. *Courtesy of Ted Patterson.*

# Other Equipment

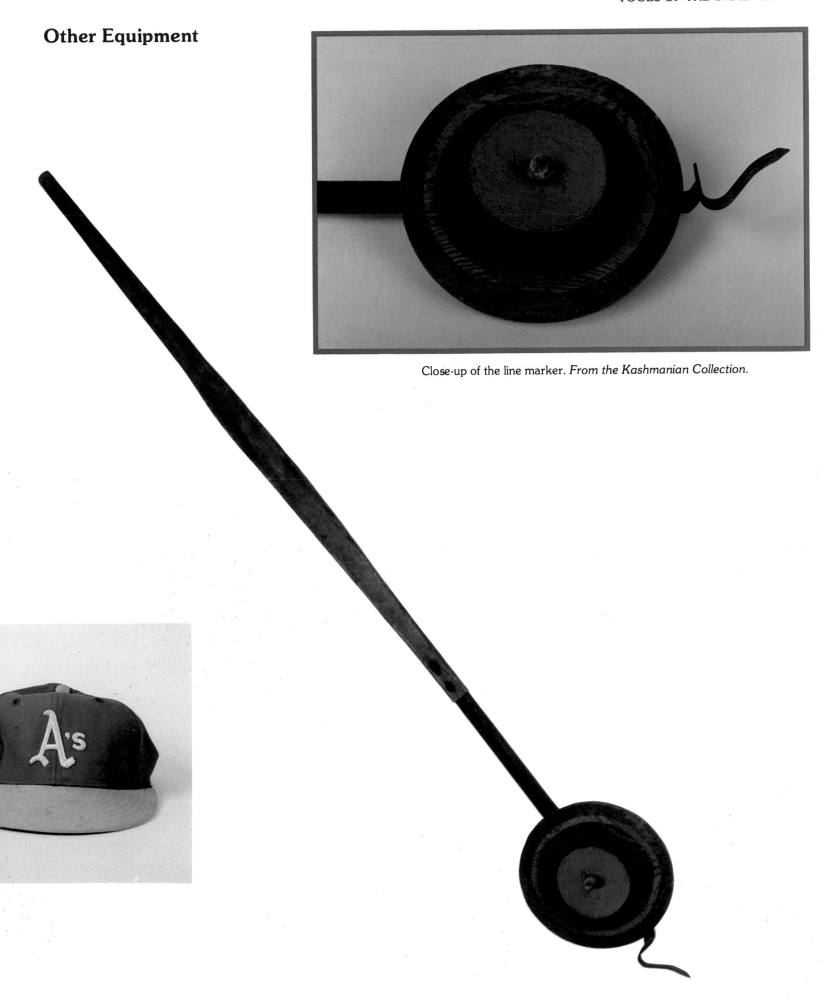

Close-up of the line marker. *From the Kashmanian Collection.*

Base Ball line marker, c. 1870-80. 53″ long. *From the Kashmanian Collection.*

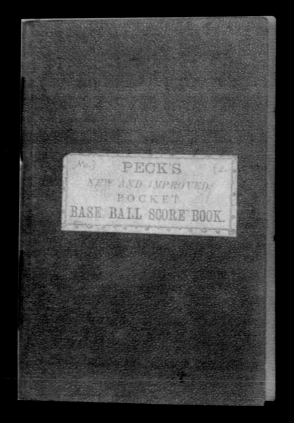

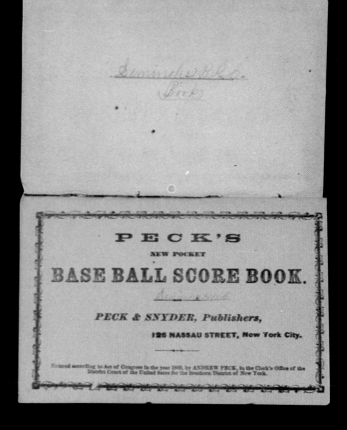

1866 score book for the Seminoles Base Ball Club. Outside
dimensions: 6″ x 4″. *From the Kashmanian Collection.*

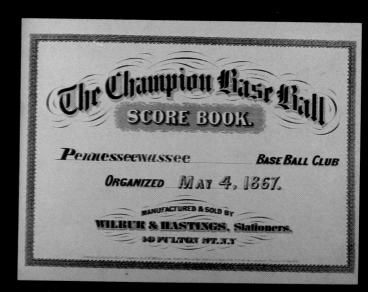

Spalding's Pocket Base Ball Score Book, printed in Chicago, c.
1884. This copy includes box scores for a Providence-Boston game
and a Chicago-Cincinnati game. *Courtesy of Baldwin's Book Barn,
West Chester, Pennsylvania.*

Score book for the Pennesseewassee Base Ball Club of Maine,
organized May 4, 1867. The book was manufactured and sold by
Wilbur & Hastings, Stationers, 40 Fulton, St. New York. 8″ x
10.75″. *From the Kashmanian Collection.*

# Chapter 5
# *Kranks and Fanatics*

Kranks, as early fans were called, gathered around baseball from the earliest days. Images of the game from the 1860s show them encircling the field, sometimes pulling their carriages around the outfield. Betting was common, and with investments riding on the game, the spectators sometimes got more involved than was healthy. One game between the Excelsior club and the Atlantics was called a draw after six innings when spectators surged onto the field to "berate players, interfere with their movements, and even prevent their recovering bounding balls." (*Baseball in America*, page 23.)

As the game moved from amateur to professional, clubs began to charge admission to help defray the expenses of the paid players. While they also sold whiskey from baskets carried through the stands, the full potential of the krank market was left to others to discover.

One of the pioneers was Harry M. Stevens, an immigrant salesman who happened into a ball park in Columbus, Ohio. When he could not tell one player from another, he had the idea of selling a score card to help the fans. He approached the owners with a proposal for printing and selling score cards with the players names printed and room for the scores. The owners asked for a $500 licensing fee, which was beyond Harry's means. In a moment of genius, however, he made a counter-offer involved the selling of advertising in the cards. They accepted and two days later Harry handed them a check for $700. The age of baseball concessions was born. (*Baseball and the American Dream*, pp. 184 ff.)

Stevens went on to create a business that is still the strongest in the field. He added food (introducing the hot dog into the lore of baseball) and souvenirs to his operations, tapping into the true fan's three basic needs: information, nourishment, and memory.

Baseball mementoes cover a broad range of interests. Even before Stevens, people in the music industry were publishing songs about the game, celebrating hero players and teams in words and music. Later, toys and games were developed that let people experience the excitement of the game in their own parlors and country stores. For the true fanatics there were

## Scorecards

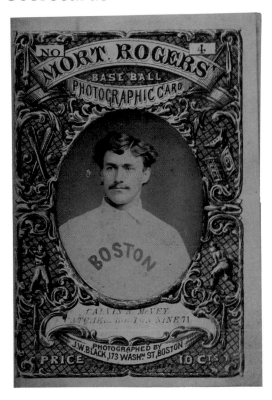

A 1871 Mort Rogers photographic scorecard with a tipped-in photo of Calvin A. McVey, catcher, Boston Nine (Red Stockings), 1871. Photographed by J. W. Black, 173 Washington Street, Boston. Published at Rogers & Fitts' Printing & Advertising House, Boston. *From the Kashmanian Collection.*

watches, salt and pepper shakers, ashtrays, pins, lapel studs, and a host of other items that could serve as a constant reminder of their obsession.

The owners knew the power of mementoes. For many years the New York Giants had sterling silver passes made for special celebrities, encouraging their attendance, and the associated publicity, at the games. The owners also knew the power of publicity. From the days of Henry Chadwick the press had been the greatest ally and supporter of the game. So, for big events like All-Star Games and World Series, they designed special pins just for the press. These are much sought after by today's collectors.

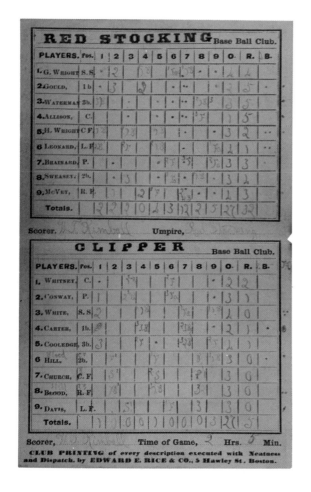

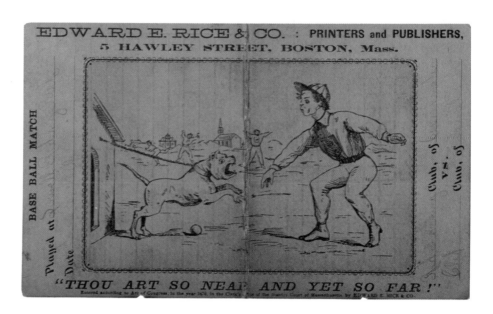

1870 scorecard for a game between the Cincinnati Red Stockings and Lowell Clippers Base Ball Club, played at the Lowell Riding Park . The game was part of the Red Stockings' famous 92 game winning streak. The players: *Cincinnati* , George Wright, Charlie Gould, Fred Waterman, Doug Allison, Harry Wright, Andy Leonard, Asa Brainard, Charlie Sweasey (sic), Cal McVey; *Lowell* , Whitney, Conway, White, Carter, Cooledge, Hill, Church, Blood, Davis. Published by Edward E. Rice & Co., Boston. *From the Kashmanian Collection.*

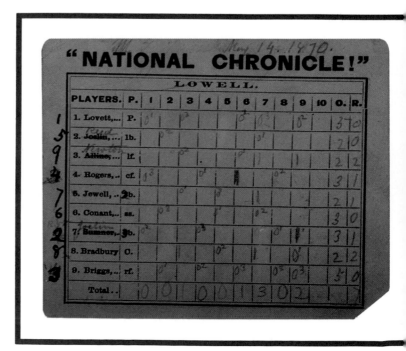

Scorecard of a game between the Forest City Base Ball Club of Cleveland and Athletic Base Ball Club of Philadelphia, c. 1870. The players: *Forest City*, Deacon White, (?) Ward, Al Pratt, Ezra Sutton, Jim Carleton, Art Allison, Gene Kimball, George Heubel, Chick Fulmer; *Philadelphia*, Al Reach, Dick McBride, Fergy Malone, Wes Fisler, Count Sensenderfer, Tom Berry, John Radcliffe, George Bechtel, Tom Pratt. Published by L.O. Rawson & Co.. *From the Kashmanian Collection.*

Score sheet for a game between Chicago and Worcester, c. 1881. Worcester, Massachusetts had a team in the National League from 1880-1882. The players: *Chicago*, Abner Dalrymple, Hugh Nicol, Mike "King" Kelly, Cap Anson, Ned Williamson, Tom Burns, Larry Corcoran, Silver Flint, Joe Quest; *Worcester*, Harry Stovey, Buttercup Dickerson, Pete Hotaling, Jerry Dorgan, Hick Carpenter, Lee Richmond, Fred Corey, George Creamer, Doc Bushong. 7.5" x 9.5". *From the Kashmanian Collection.*

Double-sided scorecard, Harvard vs. Lowell, May 14, 1870, at Jarvis Field, Harvard. 4.5 x 3.5. *From the Kashmanian Collection.*

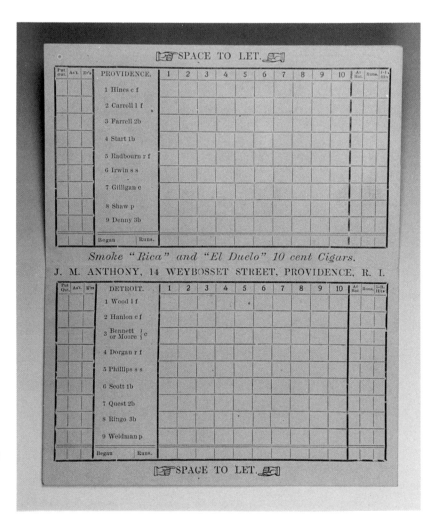

1883 National League scorecard for a game between Buffalo and New York. Buffalo was in the league from 1879-1885. The players: *Buffalo* , Curry Foley, Orator Jim O'Rourke, Deacon White, Dan Brouthers, Hardy Richardson, Orator Shaffer, Jack Rowe, Jim Lillie, Davy Force, Pud Galvin, George Derby; *New York* , Buck Ewing, Roger Connors (sic), Monte Ward, Pete Gillespie, Mike Dorgan, John Clapp, Ed Caskins (sic), Mickey Welsh (sic), Dasher Troy, Frank Hankinson. 7.5″ x 6″ unfolded. *From the Kashmanian Collection.*

Score card with nice lithographed cover published by John B. Sage, Buffalo, New York, 1885. The score card is for a game between Providence and Detroit. The players: *Providence* , Paul Hines, Cliff Carroll, Jack Farrell, Joe Start, Old Hoss Radbourn, Arthur Irwin, Barney Gilligan, Dupee Shaw, Jerry Denny; *Detroit* , George Wood, Ned Hanlon, Charlie Bennett, Jerry Moore, Jerry Dorgan, Marr Phillips, Milt Scott, Joe Quest, Frank Ringo, Stump Weidman. *Courtesy of Baldwin's Book Barn, West Chester, Pennsylvania.*

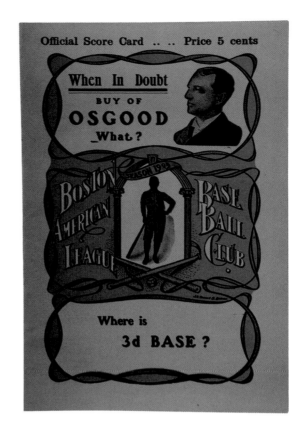

Official score card, Boston American League Base Ball Club, 1905. J.S. Conant Co, Boston. 6″ x 8.74″. From the Kashmanian Collection.

Souvenir program and score card, 1934 exhibition game, Detroit Tigers vs. St. Louis Cardinals. "Mickey" Cochrane, Manager of Detroit Tigers, on the cover. 6″ x 9.5″ folded. From the Kashmanian Collection.

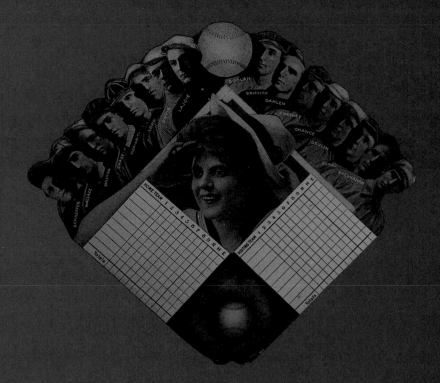

Souvenir fan, c. 1910, with Larry Doyle's photo and facsimile signature. Larry Doyle played for the New York Giants. 12″ long. *From the Kashmanian Collection.*

Fan with all-stars, c. 1910. The players: Germany Schaeffer (sic), Bobby Wallace, Billy Sullivan, Hal Chase, George Moriarity, Harry Lord, Harry Davis, Nap Lajoie, Mickey Doolan, Bill Dahlen, Bill Sweeney, Frank Chance, Art Devlin, Fred Clark (sic), Roger Bresnahan. *From the Kashmanian Collection.*

Paper fan showing managers and mascot costumes, c. 1910. The managers: *from the top* , Hughie Jennings, Detroit Tigers; Bill Dahlen, Brooklyn Bridegrooms; Patsy Donovan, Boston Red Sox; Hal Chase, New York Highlanders; Jack O'Connor, St. Louis Brownies; Connie Mack, Philadelphia White Elephants (Athletics); John McGraw, New York Giants; Clark Griffith, Cincinnati Reds; Roger Bresnahan, St. Louis Cardinals; Frank Chance, Chicago Cubs; Jimmy McAleer, Washington Senators; Deacon McGuire, Cleveland Naps; Hugh Duffy, Chicago White Sox; Fred Clarke, Pittsburgh Pirates; Red Dooin, Philadelphia Quakers; Fred Lake, Boston Braves. The other side advertises Keron's Soda, made by the Central Falls Bottling Co., Rhode Island. *From the Kashmanian Collection.*

Paper fan with baseball all-stars, c. 1910. The players: Christy Mathewson, pitcher; Hal Chase, first; Johnny Evers, second; Honus Wagner, shortstop; Harry Lord, third; Roger Bresnahan, catcher; Ty Cobb, right; Tris Speaker, center; Sherry Magee, left; Nap Lajoie at bat; Bobby Wallace running to second; Eddie Collins running to third, Mike Mitchell and Peaches Graham on deck; Johnson coaching first; Rucker coaching third; Johnstone, third base umpire; Connolly umping at home. *From the Kashmanian Collection.*

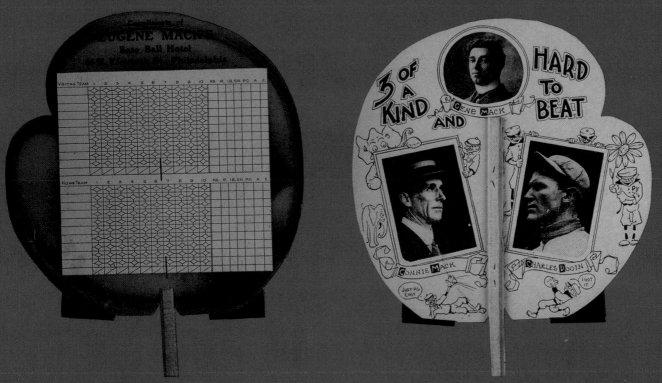

Fan, c. 1910. One side advertises Eugene Mack's Base Ball Hotel, Philadelphia. The other shows Gene Mack, Connie Mack, manager of the Philadelphia Athletics, and Charles Dooin, manager of the Philadelphia Phillies. 13" long x 8". *From the Kashmanian Collection.*

## World Series and Other Programs

Box score post card for the Pittsburgh Pirates with the results of the October 16, 1909 World Series game against Detroit recorded. 3.5" x 5.5". *From the Kashmanian Collection.*

1912 World Series program and score book, Fenway Park, Boston. 10″ x 7″. *From the Kashmanian Collection.*

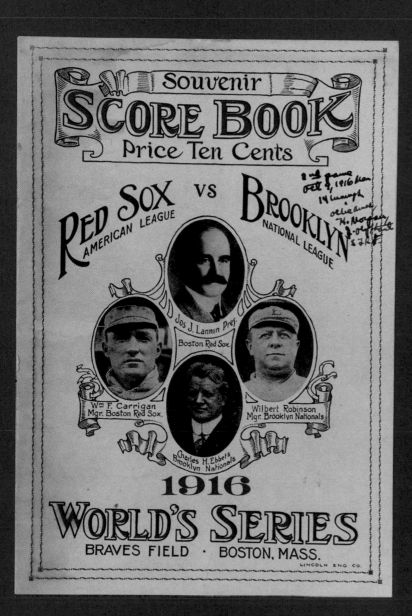

Program for 1923 World Championship Series, Yankees vs. Giants, New York City. Features managers Miller Huggins and John McGraw. The third Series in a row between the crosstown rivals, it was the first in Yankee Stadium. Previously the teams shared the Polo Grounds, with each taking turns at being the home team. It is also the first that the Yankees won. Harry M. Stevens, Publisher. 9.25″ x 11″. *From the Kashmanian Collection.*

Souvenir Score Book for the 1916 World Series, Red Sox vs. Brooklyn, Braves Field, Boston. Features managers Bill Carrigan and Wilbert Robinson, and presidents Joseph Lannin and Charles Ebbets. 7″ x 10″. *From the Kashmanian Collection.*

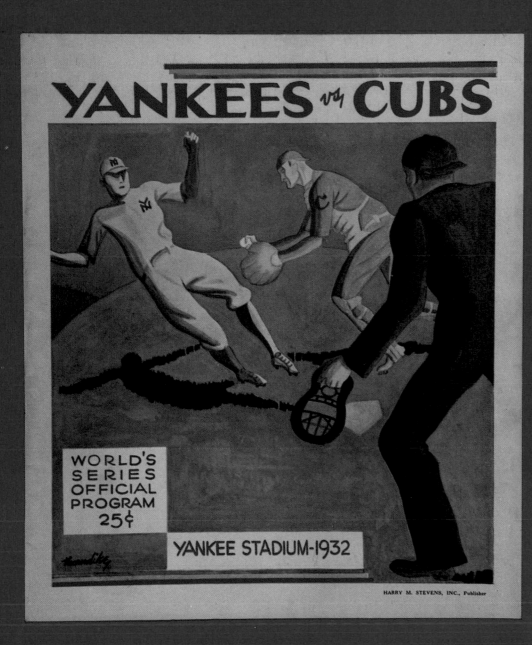

1932 World's Series Official Program, Yankees vs. Cubs. the artist
was Thorndike. Harry M. Stevens, Inc. Publisher. 9.25″ x 11″.
*From the Kashmanian Collection.*

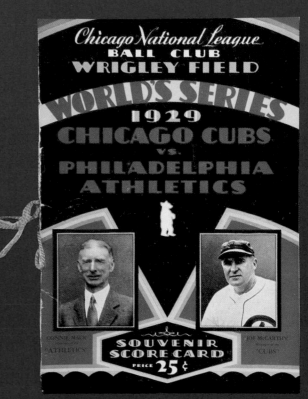

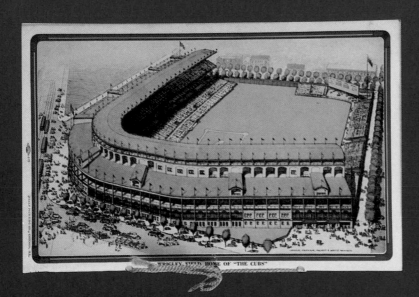

Program for 1929 World Series at Wrigley Field. 6″ x 9.25″. *From
the Kashmanian Collection.*

1940 World Series score book, Reds vs. Tigers. *From the Kashmanian Collection.*

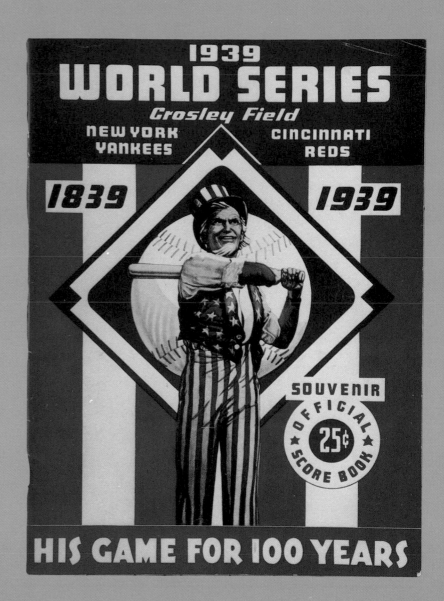

Souvenir score book for the 1939 World Series at Crosley Field, the New York Yankees versus the Cincinnati Reds. 8.5" x 11.5". *From the Kashmanian Collection.*

Negro American League Program for the 1952 International Tour. Features Indianapolis Clowns, Philadelphia Stars, Kansas City Monarchs, and the Chicago American Giants. *From the Kashmanian Collection.*

# Pennants

Red Sox 1912 American League Champions pennant. *29". From the Kashmanian Collection.*

Providence Grays, 1914 International League Champions pennant with "Smiling Bill Donovan." Babe Ruth was a member of this championship team, pitching to a 22-9 record for the summer. *29". American Pennant Mfg. Co., Providence, Rhode Island. From the Kashmanian Collection.*

Red Sox pennant, 1915. 35" x 10.5". *From the Kashmanian Collection.*

Cincinnati Redlegs pennant, thought to be from the 1930s. *From the Kashmanian Collection.*

Whiz Kid Phillies pennant, 1950s. *From the Kashmanian Collection.*

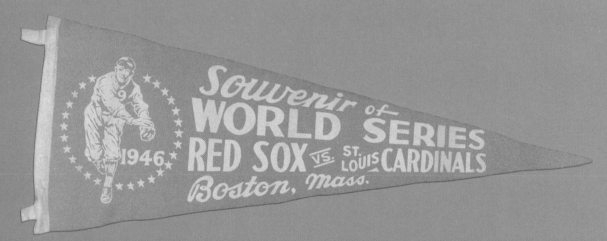

Souvenir pennant of the 1946 World Series. *From the Kashmanian Collection.*

Brooklyn Dodgers pennant, 1950s. *From the Kashmanian Collection.*

Pittsburgh Pirates pennant, 1950s. *From the Kashmanian Collection.*

New York Yankees pennant, 1950s.
*From the Kashmanian Collection.*

New York Yankees pennant,
1950s. *From the
Kashmanian Collection.*

Chicago White Sox pennant,
1950s. *From the
Kashmanian Collection.*

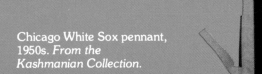

Boston Red Sox pennant, 1950s.
*From the Kashmanian Collection.*

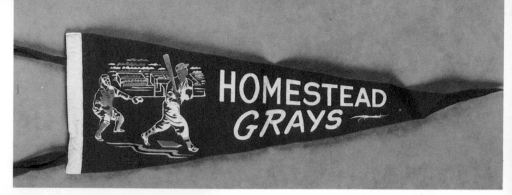

Pennant from the Negro League, Homestead Grays, Pennsylvania. 23". *From the Kashmanian Collection.*

Pennant for the Homestead Grays. 23". *From the Kashmanian Collection.*

Pennant for the Baltimore Elite Giants, Negro League. 23". *From the Kashmanian Collection.*

Pennant for the Newark Eagles, Negro League. 23". *From the Kashmanian Collection.*

Pennant for the New York Cuban Stars. 23". *From the Kashmanian Collection.*

Pennant for the New York Black Yankees. 26". *From the Kashmanian Collection.*

# Pins, Badges, and Buttons

Stick pin, 1894, saluting Baltimore, champions of the National League. 3". *From the Kashmanian Collection.*

Freddy Parent, of the Boston Americans, 1903, endorses the Cigar Makers Blue Label. 1.5". *From the Kashmanian Collection.*

Pin from Frank Chance Day, Comiskey Park, May 17. 1". *From the Kashmanian Collection.*

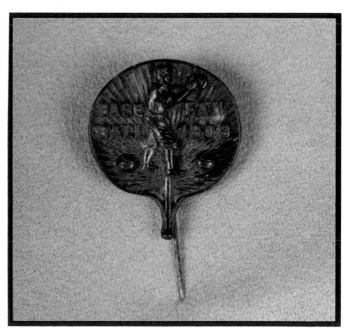

Base Ball Fan, 1909, lapel pin. *Courtesy of Mike Brown.*

Lithographed celluloid mirror with Edward J. and Stephen W. McKeever, Vice President and Second Vice President of the Brooklyn Ball Club. c. 1910-1915. 1.75" x 2.75". *From the Kashmanian Collection.*

New York press badge for Comiskey's All-American World Baseball Tour, 1914. 3.75". *From the Kashmanian Collection.*

Pin from the centennial of baseball, 1939. 3.5". *Courtesy of Mike Brown.*

Boston Braves stick pin, 1914, shaped as an Indian head. The "Miracle" Braves of 1914, had spent four of the previous five years in the national league cellar, and as late as July 18 they found themselves at the bottom of the league again. Then, with George Stallings as manager, they began their move to the top. By early September they pulled even with the perennial champs, the Giants, and by the end of the season they were 10½ games in the lead. They went on to win the World Series against the Philadelphia Athletics in a four game sweep. 1". *From the Kashmanian Collection.*

Left: Detroit Tigers brass ashtray, 4". Right: souvenir from the 1934 World Series with Mickey Cochrane and Schoolboy Rowe on the pin and a paper ball. The pin was made in Germany. *Courtesy of Mike Brown.*

Pin commemorating the Brooklyn Dodgers, National League Champions, 1952. 3.5" diam. *From the Kashmanian Collection.*

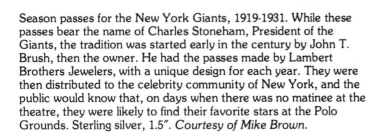

Season passes for the New York Giants, 1919-1931. While these passes bear the name of Charles Stoneham, President of the Giants, the tradition was started early in the century by John T. Brush, then the owner. He had the passes made by Lambert Brothers Jewelers, with a unique design for each year. They were then distributed to the celebrity community of New York, and the public would know that, on days when there was no matinee at the theatre, they were likely to find their favorite stars at the Polo Grounds. Sterling silver, 1.5″. *Courtesy of Mike Brown.*

1930 Boston Braves season pass, brass. 1930. 1.5″. *Courtesy of Mike Brown.*

1931 blue enamel Philadelphia Athletics press pin, .75″. *Courtesy of Mike Brown.*

1916 Brooklyn Dodgers World Series press pin, 0.5″ Made by Dieges & Clust. *Courtesy of Mike Brown.*

1932 Chicago Cubs press pin. *Courtesy of Mike Brown.*

1930 St. Louis press pin, manufactured by the St. Louis Button Company. *Courtesy of Mike Brown.*

1933 New York Giants World Series press pin. *From the Kashmanian Collection.*

1933 Washington Senators World Series press pin. *From the Kashmanian Collection.*

1935 Detroit press pin, .75". *Courtesy of Mike Brown.*

1936 New York Yankees World Series press pin. *From the Kashmanian Collection.*

1939 New York Yankees World Series press pin. *From the Kashmanian Collection.*

1943 All Star Game press pass. Plated sterling, 0.5". *Courtesy of Mike Brown.*

1945 Chicago Cubs "Victory" World Series press pin. *From the Kashmanian Collection.*

1946 All Star Game press pin, Fenway Park, Boston. *From the Kashmanian Collection.*

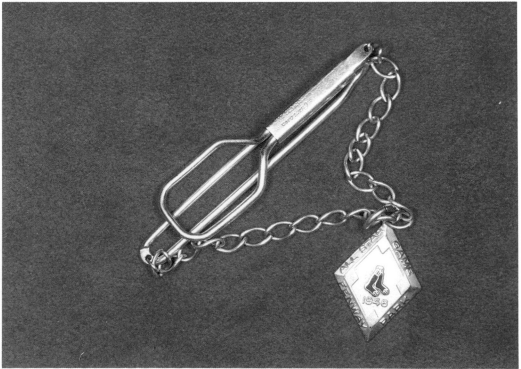

1946 All Star Game tie clip. *From the Kashmanian Collection.*

Brooklyn Dodgers World Series press pin. *From the Kashmanian Collection.*

1950 All Star Game press pin, Comiskey Park, Chicago. *From the Kashmanian Collection.*

1951 New York Yankees World Series press pin. *From the Kashmanian Collection.*

1952 New York Yankees World Series press pin. *From the Kashmanian Collection.*

1952 Brooklyn Dodgers World Series press pin. *From the Kashmanian Collection.*

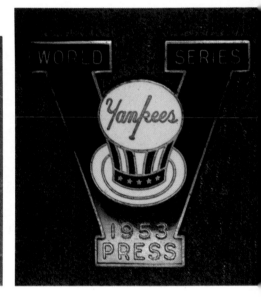

1953 New York Yankees World Series press pin. *From the Kashmanian Collection.*

1954 All Star Game press pin, Cleveland. *From the Kashmanian Collection.*

1955 Cleveland Indians World Series press pin. *From the Kashmanian Collection.*

1955 New York Yankees World Series press pin. *From the Kashmanian Collection.*

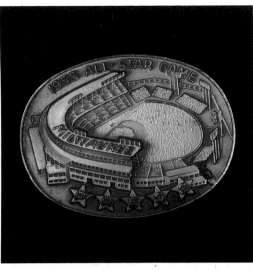

1955 All Star Game press pin, Milwaukee. *From the Kashmanian Collection.*

1956 All Star Game press pin, Washington. *From the Kashmanian Collection.*

1956 New York Yankees World Series press pin. *From the Kashmanian Collection.*

1958 All Star Game press pin, Baltimore. *From the Kashmanian Collection.*

1958 New York Yankees World Series press pin. *From the Kashmanian Collection.*

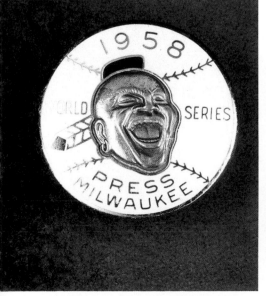

1958 Milwaukee Braves World Series press pin. *From the Kashmanian Collection.*

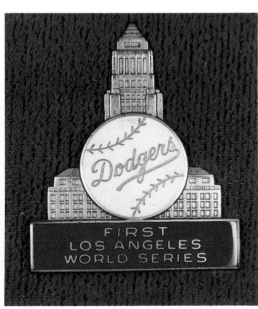

1959 Los Angeles Dodgers World Series press pin. *From the Kashmanian Collection.*

1959 Chicago White Sox World Series press pin. *From the Kashmanian Collection.*

1960 Kansas City All Star Game press pin. *From the Kashmanian Collection.*

1960 New York Yankees World Series press pin. *From the Kashmanian Collection.*

1961 San Francisco Giants All Star Game press pin. *From the Kashmanian Collection.*

1961 Cincinnati Reds World Series press pin. *From the Kashmanian Collection.*

1961 New York Yankees World Series press pin. *From the Kashmanian Collection.*

1962 All Star Game press pin, Chicago. *From the Kashmanian Collection.*

1962 San Francisco Giants World Series press pin.

1962 New York Yankees World Series press pin. *From the Kashmanian Collection.*

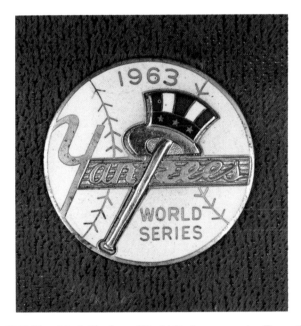

1963 New York Yankees World Series press pin. *From the Kashmanian Collection.*

1964 New York Yankees World Series press pin. *From the Kashmanian Collection.*

1967 All Star Game press pin, Anaheim. *From the Kashmanian Collection.*

1967 St. Louis Cardinals World Series press pin. *From the Kashmanian Collection.*

1968 St. Louis Cardinals World Series press pin/charm. *From the Kashmanian Collection.*

1968 All Star Game press pin, Houston. *From the Kashmanian Collection.*

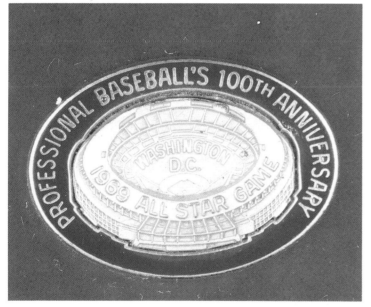

1969 All Star Game press pin, commemorating Professional Baseball's 100th Anniversary. Washington. *From the Kashmanian Collection.*

1969 New York Mets World Series press pin. *From the Kashmanian Collection.*

1972 Oakland A's World Series press pin. *From the Kashmanian Collection.*

1968 Detroit Tiger World Series press pin. *From the Kashmanian Collection.*

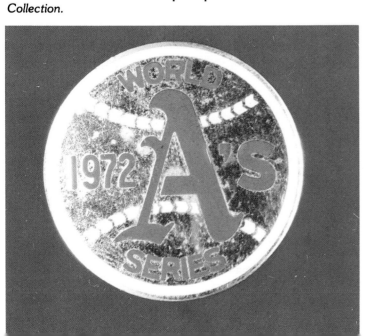

1967 Boston Red Sox World Series press pin. *From the Kashmanian Collection.*

Lapel stud of white metal featuring a pitcher, c. 1905. .75″. *Courtesy of Peg Osborne.*

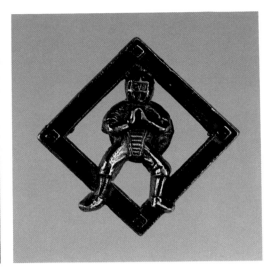

A companion piece to the pitcher stud, this lapel stud features a catcher in a diamond, c. 1905. A similar design was used in a campaign stud for Cap Anson. 1″. *Courtesy of Peg Osborne.*

Baseball shaped lapel stud for Cap Anson's campaign for Sheriff. 0.5″. *From the Kashmanian Collection.*

"I'm a Tiger Booster" lapel stud advertising the Automobile Cycle Car Co., Detroit, 1914. Silvered brass, it was made by the Green Duck Co., Chicago. .75″. *Courtesy of Peg Osborne.*

Sterling lapel stud, c. 1920s. Probably an award, it is in the shape of a baseball with the enameled initials TBL. .5″. *Courtesy of Peg Osborne.*

Chicago Playground Council lapel stud. Wm. Schridde Co., Chicago. .75″. *Courtesy of Peg Osborne.*

Lapel stud for the O.T.B.A., Old Timers Baseball Association, of Chicago. Screw back, c. 1940. .5″. *Courtesy of Peg Osborne.*

Ivory button with painted baseball design. The ball is hollow and probably contained miniature dice. It was worn on a man's waist coat, c. 1900. *Courtesy of Peg Osborne.*

Five of a set of six buttons, c. 1930s. Called "Goofies" by button collectors, they also came with green trim. .75″. *Courtesy of Peg Osborne.*

## Magazines

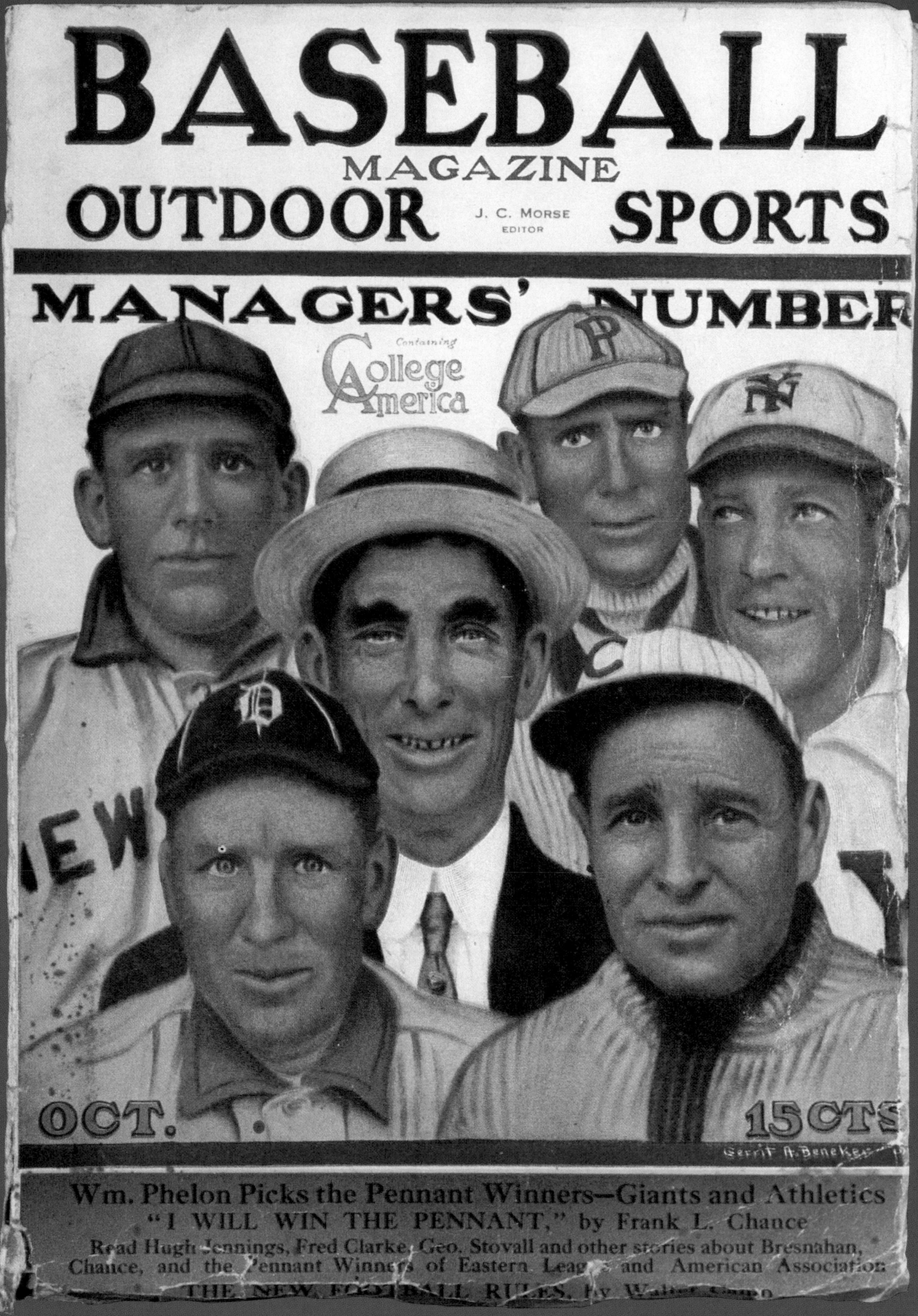

BASEBALL MAGAZINE

OUTDOOR   J. C. MORSE EDITOR   SPORTS

MANAGERS' NUMBER

Containing College America

OCT.                                    15 CTS

Wm. Phelon Picks the Pennant Winners—Giants and Athletics
"I WILL WIN THE PENNANT," by Frank L. Chance
Read Hugh Jennings, Fred Clarke, Geo. Stovall and other stories about Bresnahan,
Chance, and the Pennant Winners of Eastern League and American Association
THE NEW FOOTBALL RULES, by Walter Camp

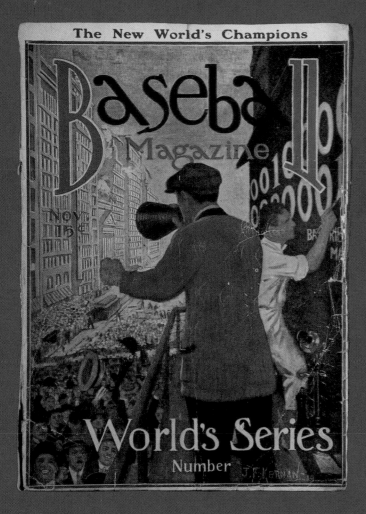

November, 1914 *Baseball Magazine* cover with art by J.F. Kernan. *From the Kashmanian Collection.*

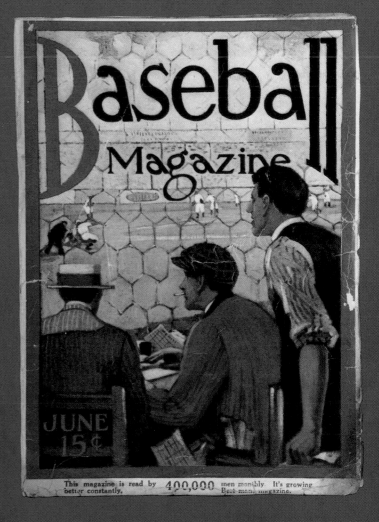

**Opposite page:**
*Baseball Magazine* cover featuring the art work of Gerrit A. Beneker. October, 1911. The managers pictured are Hal Chase, New York Highlanders; Fred Clarke, Pittsburgh; Connie Mack, Philadelphia Athletics; John McGraw, New York Giants; Hughie Jennings, Detroit; and Frank Chance, Chicago. *From the Kashmanian Collection.*

*Baseball Magazine* cover, June, 1915. The art is by J.F. Kernan. 10″ x 7″. *From the Kashmanian Collection.*

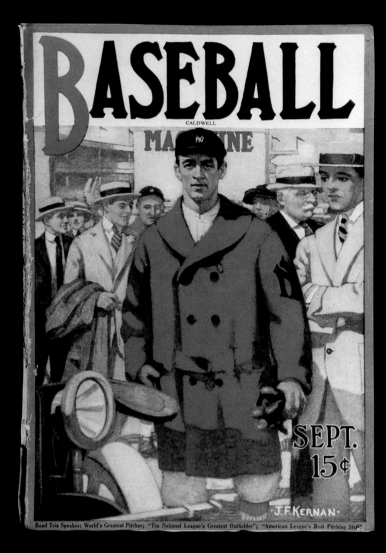

The art work of J.F. Kernan on the *Baseball Magazine* cover for September, 1916. *From the Kashmanian Collection.*

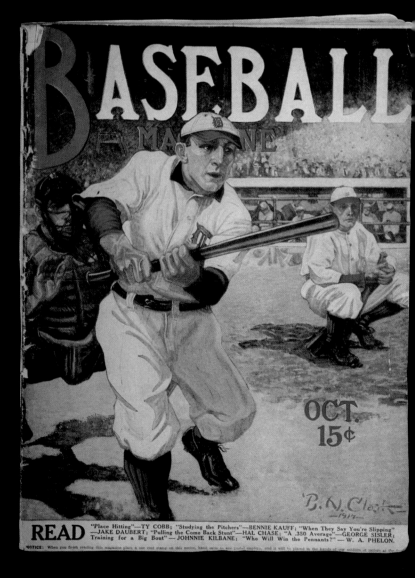

*Baseball Magazine* , 1917. B.N. Clark's rendition of Ty Cobb. 8″ x 11″. *From the Kashmanian Collection.*

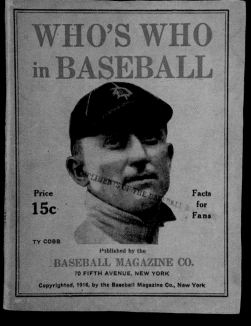

Who's Who in Baseball "Facts for Fans" with Ty Cobb. Published by the Baseball Magazine Co., 70 Fifth Ave., New York. Copyright, 1916. 4.25″ x 6.5″. *From the Kashmanian Collection.*

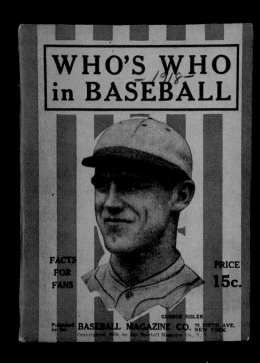

Who's Who in Baseball with George Sisler. 1918. *From the Kashmanian Collection.*

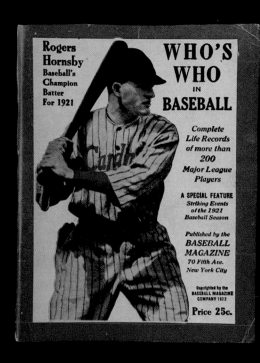

Rogers Hornsby, Baseball's Champion Batter for 1921. *Who's Who in Baseball, 1922. From the Kashmanian Collection.*

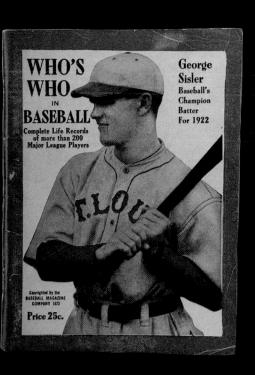

Who's Who in Baseball, 1923 with Sisler, 1922. *From the Kashmanian Collection.*

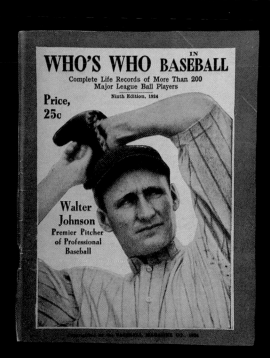

Walter Johnson, *Who's Who in Baseball*, 1924. *From the Kashmanian Collection.*

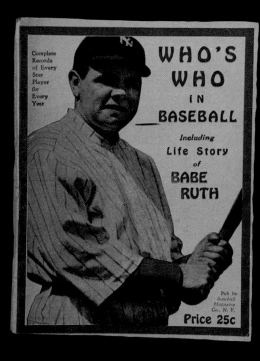

Babe Ruth, *Who's Who in Baseball*, 1921. *From the Kashmanian Collection.*

Yale—UConn football program from October 2, 1948. Inside is a picture of Ruth with George H.W. "Poppy" Bush, captain of the 1948 Yale baseball team, and, later, President of the United States. *From the Kashmanian Collection.*

A Leyendecker lithograph, probably done for a magazine originally. Paper, 25″ x 19″. *Courtesy of Ted Patterson.*

# Books

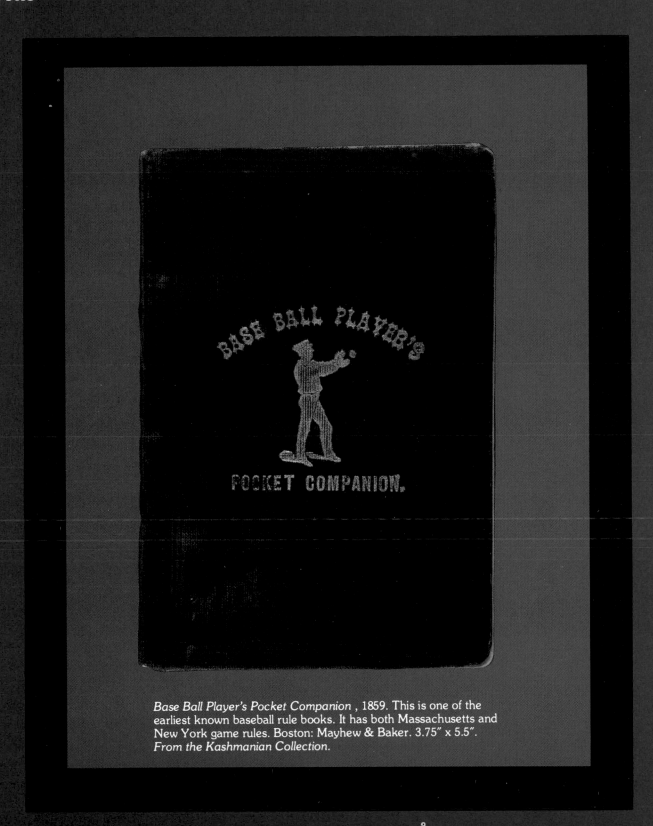

*Base Ball Player's Pocket Companion*, 1859. This is one of the earliest known baseball rule books. It has both Massachusetts and New York game rules. Boston: Mayhew & Baker. 3.75" x 5.5". *From the Kashmanian Collection.*

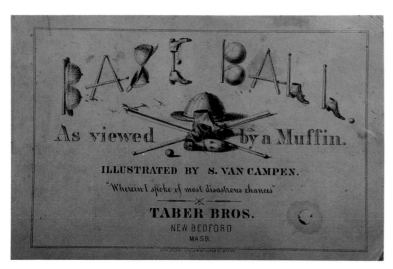

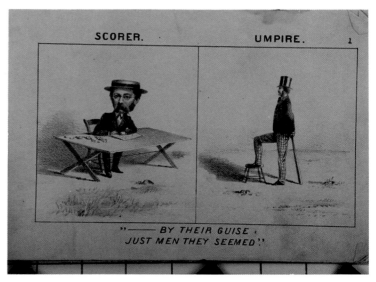

*Base Ball as Viewed by a Muffin* , illustrated by S. Van Campen. "Wherein I spoke of most disastrous chances" Taber Bros. New Bedford, Mass., Ch. H. Crosby Lith., Water St., Boston. Entered according to Act of Congress in the year 1867, by Taber Bros. This very early book about baseball looks at the sport as played by "Muffins" or amateurs. Humorous in style, it gives us an view of how the game was played. On the cover you can see the long, narrow bats, the spiked shoes, and, if you look closely, the ball sewn from six slices. 9″ x 5″. *From the Kashmanian Collection.*

The scorer and the umpire. The umpire was always supplied with a stool used more as a foot rest than a seat.

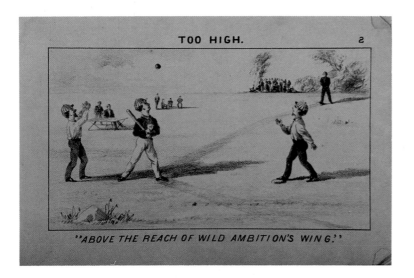

The batter had the privilege of calling the pitch he wanted. That did not always mean the pitcher would or could comply. Notice that the pitch is made underhanded.

The catcher plays from a standing position with no glove.

With no mask, the catcher is in danger not only from errant balls, but from hurled bats.

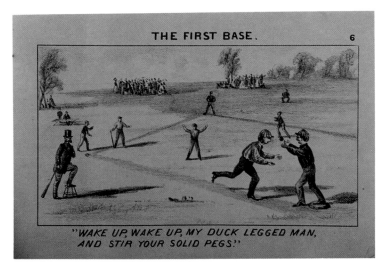

THE FIRST BASE.  6

"WAKE UP, WAKE UP, MY DUCK LEGGED MAN,
AND STIR YOUR SOLID PEGS."

The umpire, not willing to submit himself to the risks the catch takes, commonly took a position along the first base line.

"STEALING" THE SECOND BASE.  7

"THE PURPOSE YOU UNDERTAKE IS DANGEROUS."

The steal. Notice how closely the basemen stick to their bases and the shortstop playing close behind the pitcher.

AT THE THIRD BASE.  8

"CAREFUL HIS SEAT, AND CIRCUMSPECT HIS GAZE"

The slide.

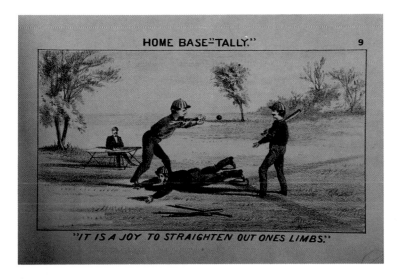

HOME BASE "TALLY."  9

"IT IS A JOY TO STRAIGHTEN OUT ONES LIMBS."

A score.

A "DAISY CUTTER."  10

"NOT LIGHTER DOES THE SWALLOW SKIM
ACROSS THE SMOOTH LAKES LEVEL BRIM."

The grounder.

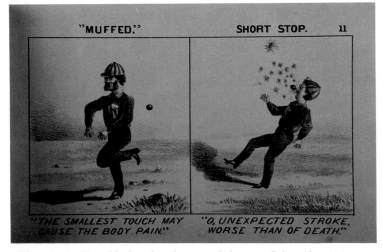

"MUFFED."    SHORT STOP.  11

"THE SMALLEST TOUCH MAY
CAUSE THE BODY PAIN"    "O, UNEXPECTED STROKE,
WORSE THAN OF DEATH."

Though the New York rules eliminated the possibility of getting a runner out by hitting him with the ball, some Muffin games still permitted it. It is not clear whether this "muffed" is an out by being hit or an error. The "short stop" needs no explanation. The early balls contained a great deal of India rubber and could take quite a bounce. In fact, a ball caught on the first bounce was at one time considered an out.

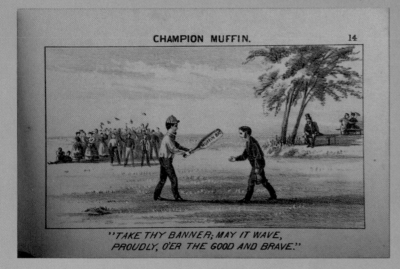

A COLLISION. 12

"WE MEET BY CHANCE."

Some things in the game have never changed, including the outfield collision.

ARNICA. 13

"WHEN THE SWALLOWS HOMEWARD FLY."
"SHORT RETIREMENT ARGUES SWEET RETURN."

After the collisions the Muffins needed a balm for their wounds. Arnica was a popular liniment for sprains and bruises, but it was not taken internally as shown in this illustration. Obviously the player has a better idea. The Muffin games were social events, and alcoholic beverages were available to fans and players alike.

CHAMPION MUFFIN. 14

"TAKE THY BANNER; MAY IT WAVE,
PROUDLY, O'ER THE GOOD AND BRAVE."

The champion in this game was awarded the "Muffin Bat," which bears a strong resemblance to a cricket bat.

FLY CATCH. HOME RUN. 15

"AND NEARER, CLEARER, DEADLIER
THAN BEFORE."

"ENOUGH!I SOUGHT TO DRIVE AWAY
THE LAZY HOURS OF PEACEFUL DAY."

The home run here is the long, painful trip home after the game.

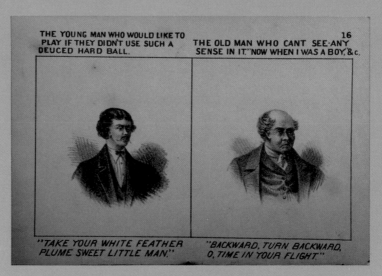

THE YOUNG MAN WHO WOULD LIKE TO
PLAY IF THEY DIDN'T USE SUCH A
DEUCED HARD BALL.

THE OLD MAN WHO CANT SEE ANY
SENSE IN IT. "NOW WHEN I WAS A BOY, &c. 16

"TAKE YOUR WHITE FEATHER
PLUME SWEET LITTLE MAN."

"BACKWARD, TURN BACKWARD,
O, TIME IN YOUR FLIGHT."

Final observations.

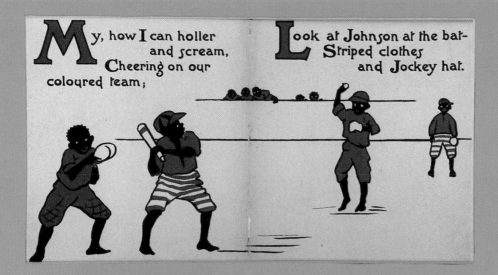

Illustrated pages from a child's book. 12″ x 6.5″. *From the Kashmanian Collection.*

*Spalding's Official Base Ball Guides* from 1880, 1881, and 1885. A.G. Spalding & Co., Chicago. The annual guides contained rules, reviews of the previous season, and statistics. *Courtesy of Baldwin's Book Barn, West Chester, Pennsylvania.*

*Spalding's Official Base Ball Guides* from 1889, 1891, 1892. *Courtesy of Baldwin's Book Barn, West Chester, Pennsylvania.*

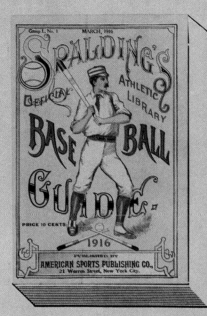

*The Official Book of Base Ball* poster, 1916. Spalding's official book was published by American Sports Publishing Co. 21.75" x 13.75". *Courtesy of Ted Patterson.*

*Reach's Official American Association Base Ball Guide* from 1888 and 1889. A.J. Reach Co., Philadelphia, Pennsylvania. *Courtesy of Baldwin's Book Barn, West Chester, Pennsylvania.*

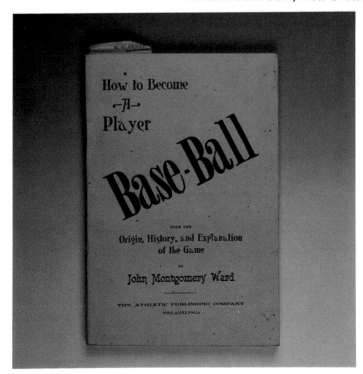

*Base-Ball: How to Become a Player*, by John Montgomery Ward, Athletic Publishing Co., Philadelphia, 1888. *Courtesy of Baldwin's Book Barn, West Chester, Pennsylvania.*

*"Play Ball": Stories of the Ball Field,* Mike "King" Kelly. Published by Emory & Hughes, Boston, 1888. *Courtesy of Baldwin's Book Barn, West Chester, Pennsylvania.*

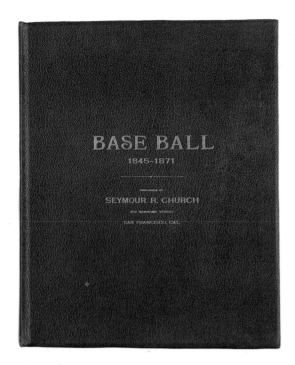

Cover of *Base Ball, 1845-1871* . Published by Seymour R. Church, San Francisco, California, copyright 1902. 11″ x 14″. *From the Kashmanian Collection.*

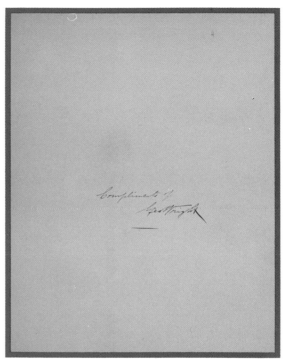

Autograph of George Wright. *From the Kashmanian Collection.*

Color lithograph of Cal A. McVey, to whom the book was dedicated. Artist: Carl Dahlgren, plates by Bolton & Strong. *From the Kashmanian Collection.*

Color lithograph of George Wright and the Golden Gate. Carl
Dahlgren, artist, plates by Bolton & Strong. Three color press
work by Walter N. Brunt. *From the Kashmanian Collection.*

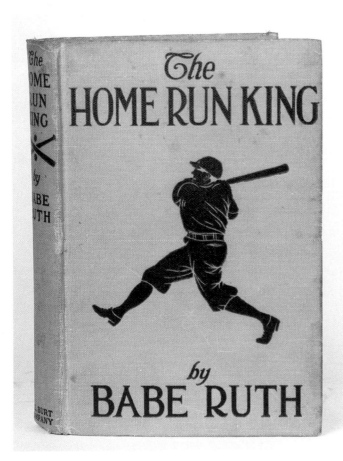

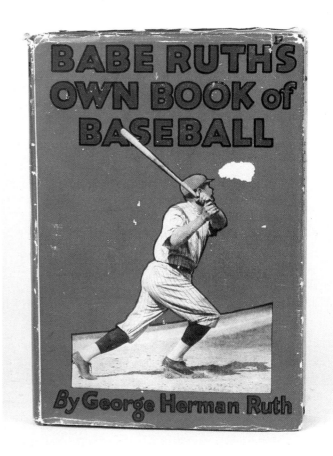

*The Home Run King* , Babe Ruth. A children's novel with loose
reference to Babe Ruth's life. A.L. Burt Company, New York,
1920. *From the Kashmanian Collection.*

*Babe Ruth's Own Book of Baseball* , George Herman Ruth.
Published by A.L. Burt, 1922. *From the Kashmanian Collection.*

## Sheet Music

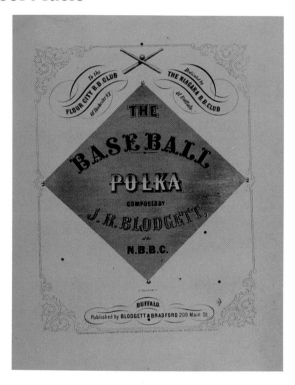

"The Base Ball Polka." composed by J.R. Blodgett of the N.B.B.C. (Niagara Base Ball Club), J. Sage & Sons, 1858. This is the first reference to Base Ball in sheet music, and the beginning of many baseball related tunes. Dedicated to the Flour City Base Ball Club of Rochester, New York by the N.B.B.C. of Buffalo. Published by Blodgett & Bradford, Buffalo. 10″ x 13.5″. *From the Kashmanian Collection.*

The cover of "The Live Oak Polka," 1860, is the first time a baseball image appeared on sheet music. Composed by J.H. Kalbfleisch and dedicated to the Live Oak B.B.C., Rochester, New York, the cover was lithographed at Endicott & Co. Lith. New York. Published by Jos. P. Shaw, Rochester. 14″ x 11″. *From the Kashmanian Collection.*

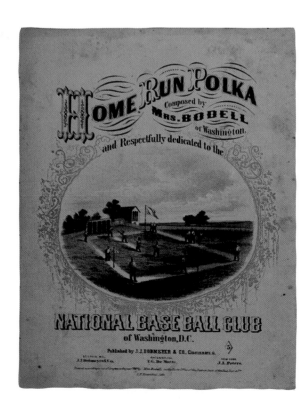

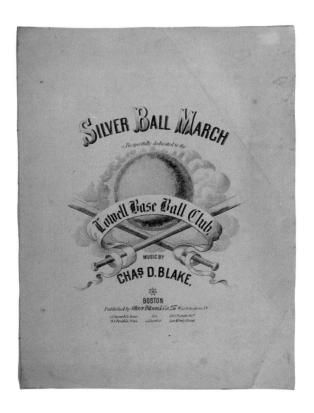

"Home Run Polka" composed by Mrs. Bodell of Washington and dedicated to the National Base Ball Club of Washington, D.C. Published by J.J. Dobmeyer & Co., Cincinnatti, 1867. The image here is of base ball played by the Massachusetts rules with the batting area located midway between the bases. Lithography by L.N. Rosenthal Lith. 10.75″ x 14″. *From the Kashmanian Collection.*

"Silver Ball March," the Lowell Base Ball Club of Boston. Published by Oliver Ditson & Co. Washington St., Cincinnati. 10.5″ x 14″. *From the Kashmanian Collection.*

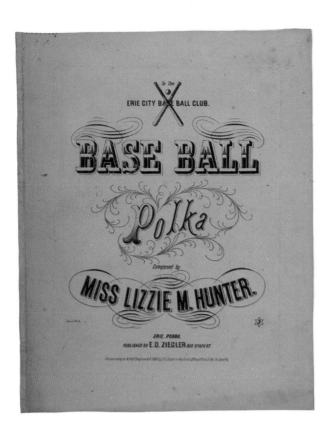

Erie City Base Ball Club "Base Ball Polka," composed by Miss Lizzie M. Hunter. Published by E.D. Ziegler, Erie, Pennsylvania, 1868. 10.5" x 13.5". *From the Kashmanian Collection.*

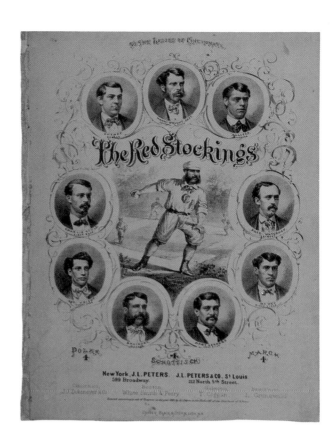

"The Red Stockings Polka," saluting the first professional base ball club, the Cincinnati Red Stockings. The players (clockwise from the top center): Harry Wright, Captain, Doug Allison, Fred Waterman, Cal McVey, Andy Leonard, Asa Brainard, George Wright, Charlie Gould, Charlie Sweasy. In the center Brainard is pitching. Published by J.L. Peters, Broadway, New York, 1869. Lithography by Snyder, Black & Sturn, Lith. New York. 10" x 13.75". *From the Kashmanian Collection.*

"Boston Americans March," featuring Captain Jimmy Collins, now a Hall of Famer, 1903. 10.5" x 14". *From the Kashmanian Collection.*

"Base Ball Galop" sheet music, 1885. Composed by B. Immer. Tipped in photo of the Lyon & Healy Baseball Club, Chicago. Published by Diston & Co. 10.75" x 13.5". *From the Kashmanian Collection.*

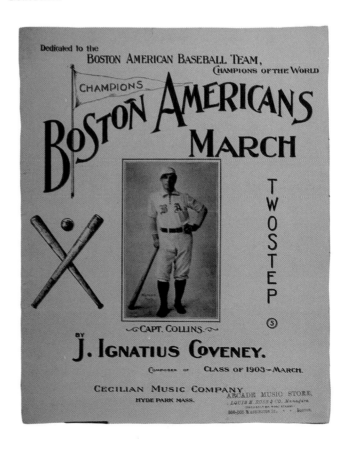

"The White Sox March" by T.F. Durand, composer of "Twinkling Stars." Dedicated to Charles A. Comiskey, who was the owner of the 1906 World Champion Chicago White Sox, "The Hitless Wonders." Tomaz F. Deuther, Music Publisher, Chicago, Illinois, 1907. *From the Kashmanian Collection.*

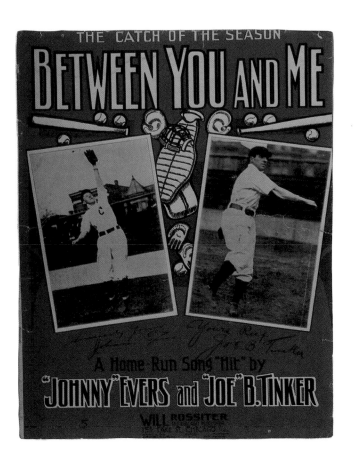

Sheet music of "Between You and Me," with Johnny Evers and Joe Tinker on the cover. Will Rossiter, "The Chicago Publisher," 1908. 10″ x 13.5″. *From the Kashmanian Collection.*

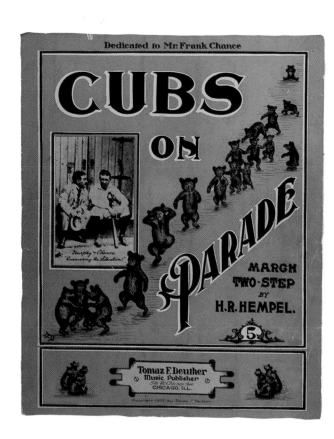

"Cubs on Parade." Features Murphy and Frank Chance. Tomaz F. Deuther, Music Publisher, Chicago, Illinois, 1907. *From the Kashmanian Collection.*

Sheet music for "Oh You Tigers," a song saluting the Detroit Tigers, American League pennant winner. Published by Anna M. De Varennes. Bay City, Mich. Copyrighted 1909. 11″ x 13.5″. *From the Kashmanian Collection.*

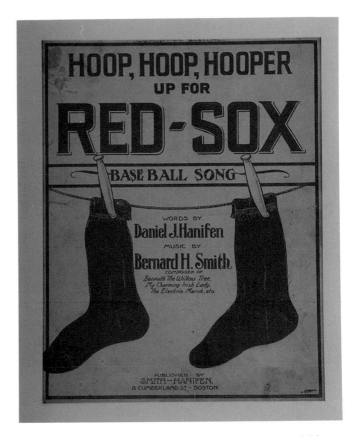

Sheet music presenting the 1912 International League champions, the Rochester Hustlers. Published by Harry Abramson "The Rochester Publisher," Glenny Bldg., Rochester, New York. 11″ x 14″. *From the Kashmanian Collection.*

"Hoop, Hoop, Hooper Up for Red Sox: Base Ball Song." Music saluted Harry Hooper, Hall of Fame Red Sox outfielder. Published by Smith-Hanifen, Boston, c. 1912. *From the Kashmanian Collection.*

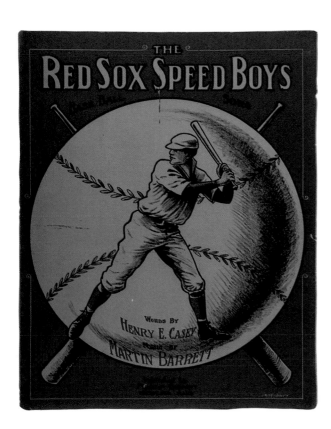

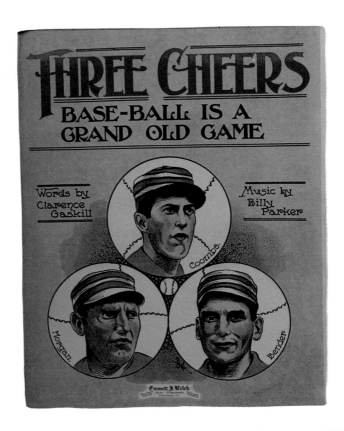

"The Red Sox Speed Boys." Published by Martin Barrett, Brookline, Massachusetts, 1912. Artist, E.S. Fisher. 10.5″ x 14″. *From the Kashmanian Collection.*

"Three Cheers Base-Ball Is a Grand Old Game" sheet music. Chief Bender, Jack Coombs, and Cy Morgan pitched for the Philadelphia Athletics. Emmett F. Welch, Music Publisher, Philadelphia ,Pennsylvania, 1912. *From the Kashmanian Collection.*

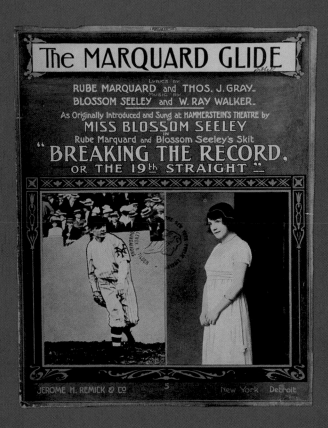

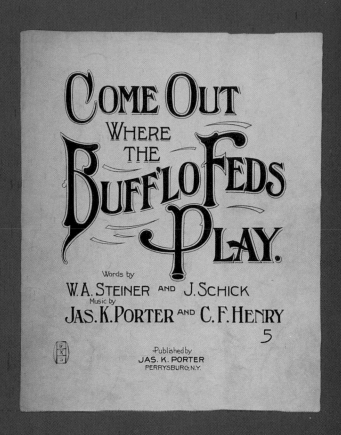

"The Marquard Glide" sheet music. Rube Marquard won 19 straight games and wrote this song to commemorate the event. He performed it with his wife, Blossom Seeley, a well-known vaudevillian singer, in a skit called "Breaking the Record." Jerome H. Remick & Co. New York, Detroit, 1912. *From the Kashmanian Collection.*

"Come Out Where the Buffalo Feds Play," sheet music, c. 1914. Buffalo was a member of the short-lived Federal League, 1914-15. Published by Jas. K. Porter, Perrysburg, New York. 10.75 x 13.75. *From the Kashmanian Collection.*

"Oh! You Babe Ruth" sheet music. Snyder Service, New York, 1920. 9.5" x 12.5". *From the Kashmanian Collection.*

"The Cincinnati Reds Song," 1919. The 1919 Reds were World Champions and participants in the infamous Black Sox World Series. Olympic Music Publishers, Cincinnati. *From the Kashmanian Collection.*

"Babe Ruth! Babe Ruth! (We Know What He Can Do)," sheet music published by J.W. Spencer, Olneyville, Rhode Island, late 1920s. 12" x 9.25". *Courtesy of Ted Patterson.*

# For the Home and Office

Salt cellars. Left to right: Knickerbocker Silver Company, Quadrupleplate, 2.25"; unmarked, 3.25"; unmarked, 2.25". *Courtesy of Mike Brown.*

1939 Hall of Fame salt and pepper. Silver plate, 2.25". Made in Japan. *Courtesy of Mike Brown.*

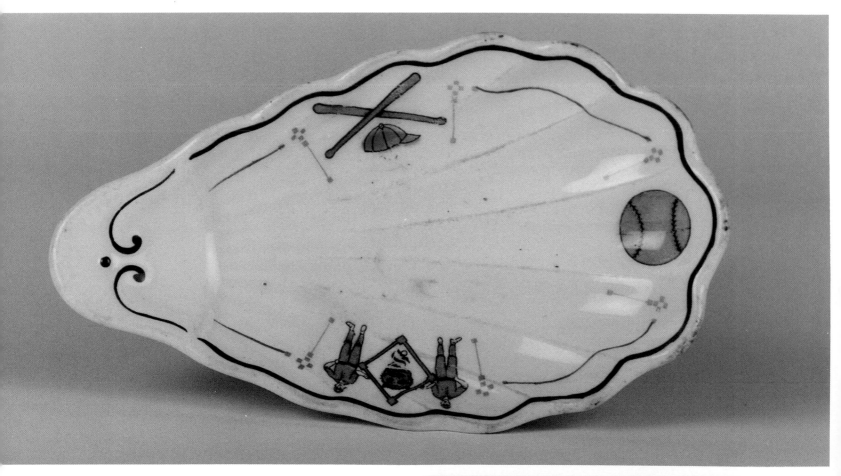

Candy dish souvenir from the Detroit Tigers, Shenango Pottery Co., New Castle, Pennsylvania, c. 1912. 8" x 4.5". *Courtesy of Mike Brown.*

Cast pewter candy dish, 3.25" x 4" x 2". It had a screw top which made it into a bank. *Courtesy of Mike Brown.*

Paper box, probably for candy, with composition figure. 4" x 3.75". *Courtesy of Mike Brown.*

Candy container, papier mâché with wood stick. 7" x 3". *Courtesy of Mike Brown.*

Pewter bookends, c. 1915. 6.5". *Courtesy of Mike Brown.*

1939 Hall of Fame souvenirs. Left: paper weight, 2″ x 5″ x 4″; right: copper letter opener, 2″ x 9″. National Baseball Museum and Hall of Fame on plagues. *Courtesy of Mike Brown.*

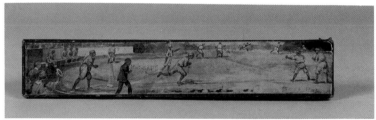

Pencil box. Cardboard, 1.75″ x 9.5″ x 0.5″. *Courtesy of Mike Brown.*

Inkwell, Japan, c. 1930s. 3.5″. *Courtesy of Mike Brown.*

Baseball lighters. Left: Kent, Japan, with crossed bats on back; right: marked L-S-M-C, Japan. 2″ x 1.5″. *Courtesy of Mike Brown.*

Silver-plated match safe, c. 1890. *Courtesy of Mike Brown.*

Lighter, marked CMC New York. Silver plated, Japan. 3.25 x 2.25 *Courtesy of Mike Brown.*

Cubs ashtray, cast aluminum, c. 1910. 6 x 4.5″ x 6.5″. *Courtesy of Mike Brown.*

Souvenir ashtray, Bill's, Milwaukee., c. 1930-35. *Courtesy of Mike Brown.*

Baseball-and-bat briar pipe, 2″ x 4″, with metal pipe stand. *Courtesy of Mike Brown.*

Harris belt featuring Babe Ruth on the buckle, c. 1930s. Buckle: 2" x 1". *From the Kashmanian Collection.*

Watch fob, steel, 2.75". *Courtesy of Mike Brown.*

Brass on marble watch fob, c. 1910. *Courtesy of Mike Brown.*

"Ty Cobb" watch fob, advertising Elastica Floor Finish, c. 1910. *Courtesy of Mike Brown.*

Brass lady's card case, 2.25″ x 1.5″. *Courtesy of Mike Brown.*

Babe Ruth pocket knife. Bakelite. 2.5″. *From the Kashmanian Collection.*

Ty Cobb's pocketknife given to the author by a biographer of Cobb. 4″. *From the Kashmanian Collection.*

Dizzy Dean wristwatch, 1935. Made by Everbrite, this is the first baseball player watch. *Courtesy of Hy Brown.*

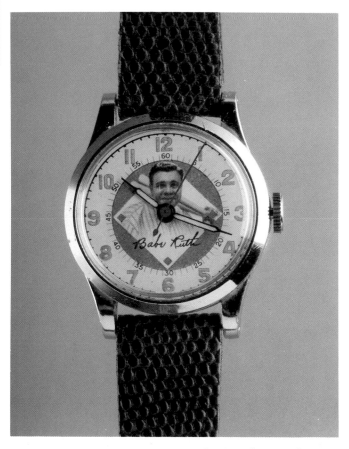

Babe Ruth wristwatch by Exacta, 1949. Came with a metal expansion band and was packaged in a plastic baseball. *Courtesy of Hy Brown.*

Tie rack. 6.5″ x 11″. *Courtesy of Mike Brown.*

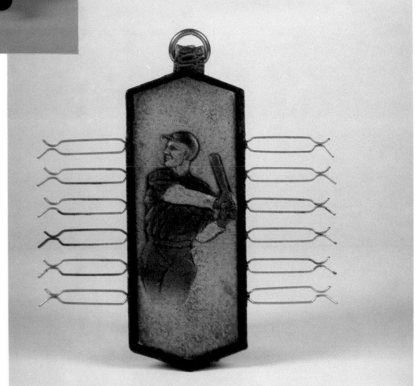

Embossed leather and steel tie rack. 6.75″ x 5.75″. *Courtesy of Mike Brown.*

Ceramic mug commemorating the World Champion Braves of 1914. On the back is written: "Stallings, Mgr., Evers, 2nd B., Capt." 5″. *From the Kashmanian Collection.*

Three ceramic mugs. Occupied Japan, 4″ x 3″. *Courtesy of Mike Brown.*

Plate, 6.25", and cereal bowl, 7". *Courtesy of Mike Brown.*

Porcelain bowl. Marked M & Z, Austria. 4" x 9" x 8". Probably dates to the 1940s. *Courtesy of Mike Brown.*

Bavarian porcelain, c. 1909, Forbes Field Champion Pirates Baseball Park, Pittsburgh, Pennsylvania. *Courtesy of Mike Brown.*

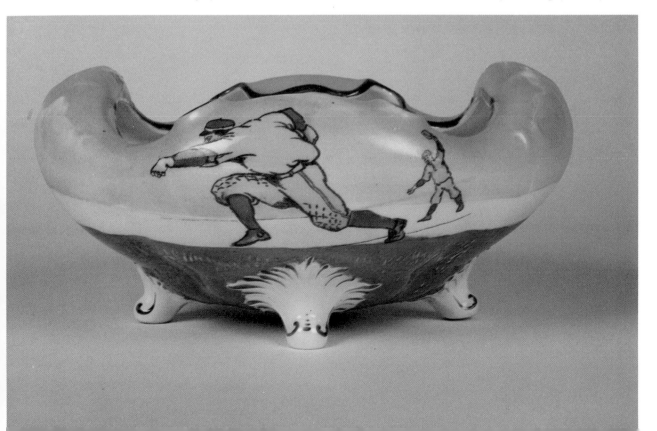

Ceramic baseball bank with Babe Ruth. Manufacturer unknown. 4". *From the Kashmanian Collection.*

Assorted ceramic pieces using the baseball theme. Left to right: salt and pepper; inkwell; ashtray in ball with matchholder on back; ashtray with matchsafe. Made in Japan, c. 1930-35. *Courtesy of Mike Brown.*

Pottery perfume bottle. 2.75″ x 1″ x 0.5″. The top may or may not be original. *Courtesy of Mike Brown.*

Wood incense burner, 6″. *Courtesy of Mike Brown.*

German bisque cigar flicker, 3.5″ x 2″. *Courtesy of Mike Brown.*

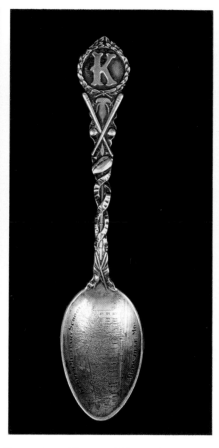

Sterling spoon from Hot Springs, Arkansas. 5″. *Courtesy of Mike Brown.*

Cornell University sterling spoon, 6″. *Courtesy of Mike Brown.*

Spoon from Kemper Military School, Boonville, Missouri. Sterling, 6″. *Courtesy of Mike Brown.*

Sterling spoon from Yale University, 6″. *Courtesy of Mike Brown.*

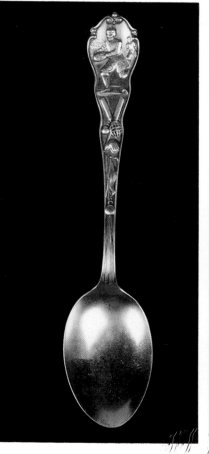

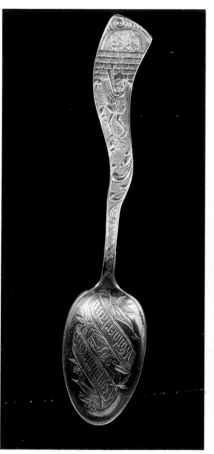
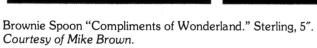

Sterling all-sports spoon, 5.5″. *Courtesy of Mike Brown.*

Spoon from the Music Hall, Cincinnatti, Ohio. Sterling, 5.5″. *Courtesy of Mike Brown.*

Brownie Spoon "Compliments of Wonderland." Sterling, 5″. *Courtesy of Mike Brown.*

Lehigh University sterling spoon, 4.25″. *Courtesy of Mike Brown.*

Base for gas lamp fixture. The flame comes up behind player. The "H" is for Hartford. Cast iron, 1876. 7".
*From the Kashmanian Collection.*

Base for a gas lamp fixture. The player is in a pitcher's pose, and the flame rises up behind the player. A "C" for Chicago is on the chest and reference to the Chicago Club is on the belt. Cast iron, 1876. 7". *From the Kashmanian Collection.*

# Coin-Operated Games

Candy dispensing game, c. 1920. Inserting one penny causes the gum ball to drop. The player tries to catch it with the fielder. If he succeeds he gets two pieces of gum, if not he still gets one. 23" x 16" x 7.5". *Courtesy of Mike Brown.*

Coin operated gumball game, c. 1920. Insert a penny and the gum falls down and becomes a game piece. After play the gum ball comes down the slot. If a home run is made, the owner is called and the player receives a prize. *Courtesy of Mike Brown.*

"Hercules Midget Baseball" coin operated game. Hercules Novelty, Chicago. 21″ x 14.5″ x 7″. *Courtesy of Mike Brown.*

"Midget Baseball" coin operated game. Wood and metal, 16″ x 9.5″ x 7.5″. *Courtesy of Mike Brown.*

"Major Series," RMC Rock-ola Product. 18″ x 13″ x 9″. *Courtesy of Mike Brown.*

"Miniature Baseball, World Champion" coin operated game. Wood and metal, 16″ x 10″ x 9″. *Courtesy of Mike Brown.*

"Base Ball" coin operated game. Wood and metal, 13″ x 12″ x 7.5″. *Courtesy of Mike Brown.*

"Play Ball Amusement Machine," Exhibit Supply Co., Chicago. 18″ x 12″ x 7″. *Courtesy of Mike Brown.*

"Baseball Ball Gum" slot machine, O.D. Jennings & Company, Chicago. 16" x 11" x 8". *Courtesy of Mike Brown.*

"Home Run Pinball Game," 10 Balls for 5 cents, late 1920s -early 1930s. *Courtesy of Ted Patterson.*

Exhibit cards by Exhibit Supply Co., Chicago, Illinois, c. 1920s & 1930s, with an advertising poster and machine. The cost was one cent per card. *Courtesy of Ted Patterson.*

# Toys and Games

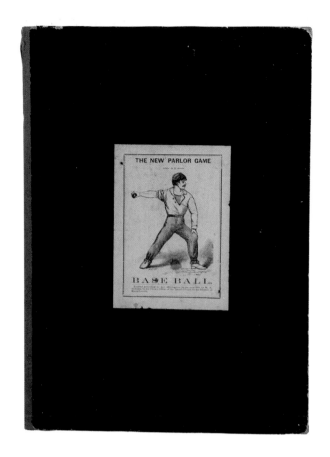

The first known base ball board game, "The New Parlor Game of Base Ball," was copyrighted in 1869 by M.B. Sumner. Outside and inside views. Printed by Bufford's Lith. 490 Washington St. Boston. 8.5″ x 12″ folded. *From the Kashmanian Collection.*

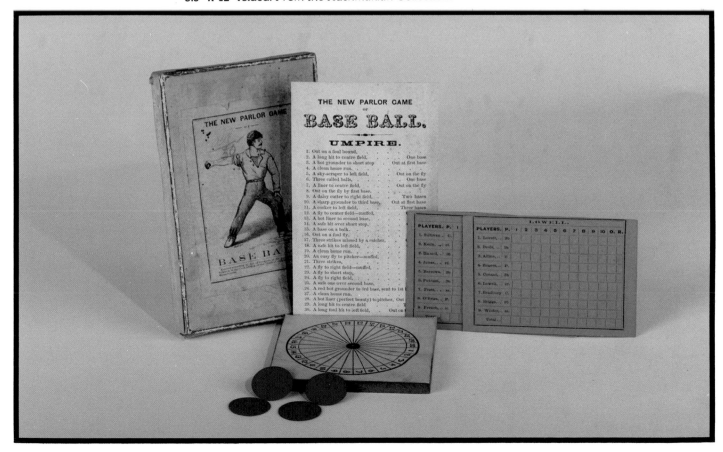

Playing pieces for "The New Parlor Game of Base Ball." 6.75″ x 4.25″ x .75″. *From the Kashmanian Collection.*

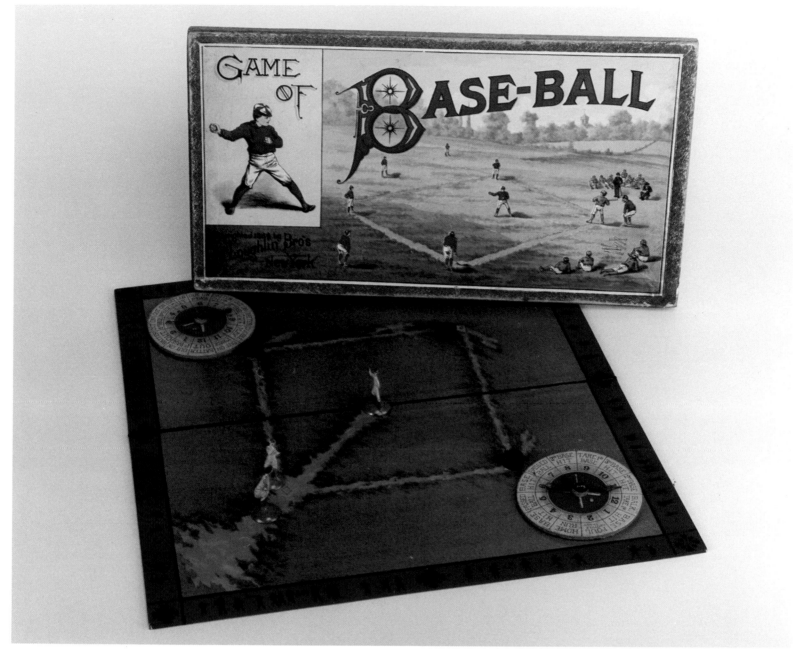

"Base-Ball" game with directions, McLoughlin Bros., New York, copyright 1886. 17.5″ x 9″. Lead player pieces, 1.5″. *From the Kashmanian Collection.*

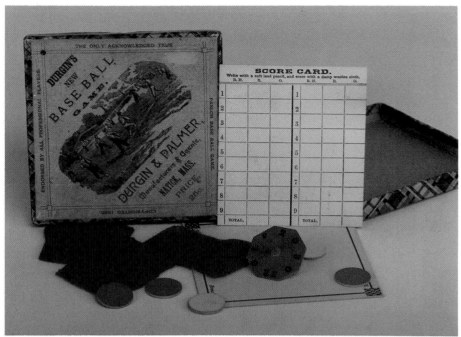

"Durgin's New Base Ball Game." Durgin & Palmer, Manufacturers
& Agents, Natick, Massachusetts, copyright 1885. The cloth is
used to erase the scoreboard. 4″ x 4.5″. *From the Kashmanian
Collection.*

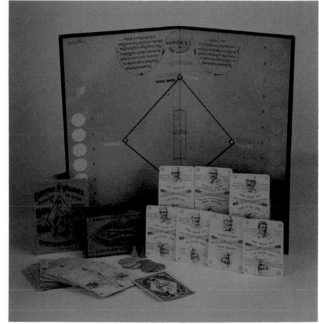

Easily played "Egerton R. Williams Popular Indoor Base Ball
Game," copyright 1889. The board is 15″ x 14″.

A close-up view of the cards. Top row, left to right: Monte Ward,
Pud Galvin, Mike "King" Kelly; bottom row, left to right: Pop
Corkhill, Dan Brouthers, Cap Anson, Charlie Comiskey. *From the
Kashmanian Collection.*

Game pieces from a mechanical board game, late 1800s. Pitcher
and batter were spring loaded. 3.25". *Courtesy of Mike Brown.*

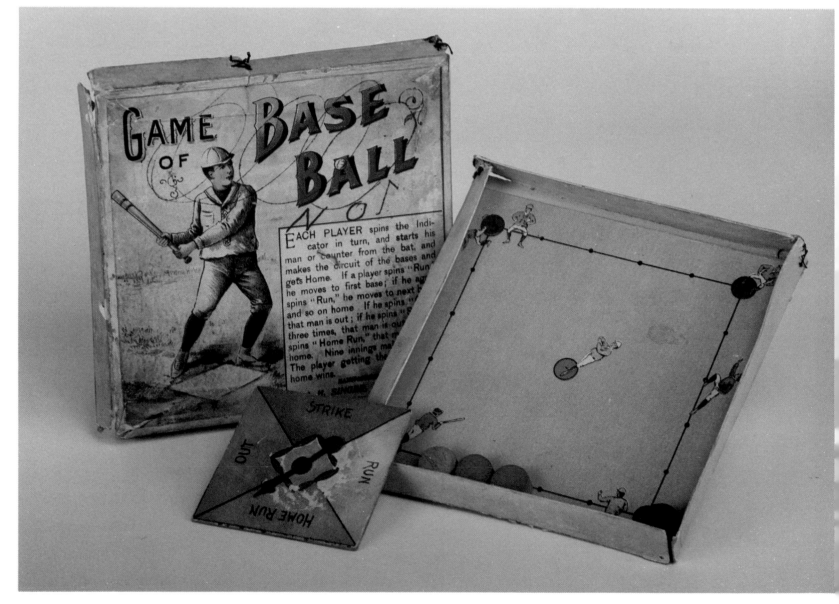

"Game of Base Ball," manufactured by J.H. Singer, New York.
5.25" x 5.25". *From the Kashmanian Collection.*

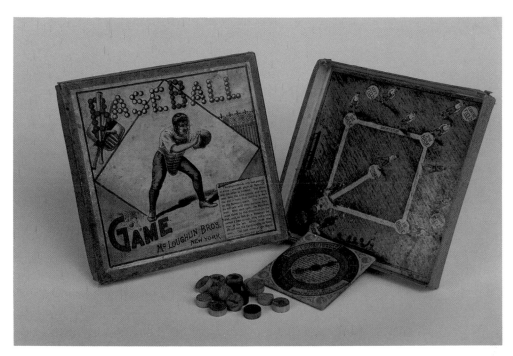

"Base Ball Game," McLoughlin Bros., New York. Directions are attached to lid. 7.5″ x 7/5″. *From the Kashmanian Collection.*

"Base Ball," George Norris Co., Boston, Massachusetts, c. 1905 *Courtesy of Mike Brown.*

"National Base Ball Puzzle," Popular Games Co., New York. "The trick, Hold 'Matty' in box while Evers makes a home run, without running off diamond." 3″. *From the Kashmanian Collection.*

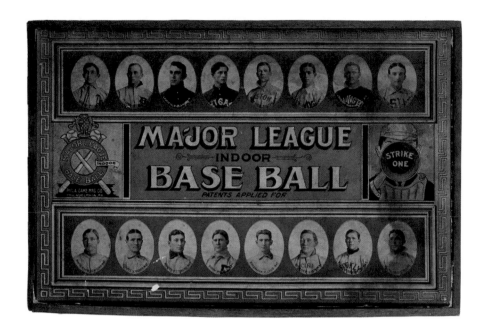

"Major League Indoor Base Ball" game. Philadelphia Game Mfg. Co., Phila., c. 1912. The players: *top row*, Home Run Baker, Ty Cobb, Nap Lajoie, Ed Walsh, Tris Speaker, Hal Chase, Walter Johnson, Bobby Wallace; *bottom row*, Christy Mathewson, Frank Chance, Honus Wagner, Red Dooin, Roger Bresnahan, Bob Bescher, Nap Rucker, Johnny Kling. 19″ x 13.5″ x 3″. Wood and cardboard. *From the Kashmanian Collection.*

Early edition of "Our National Game," c. 1915. *Courtesy of Mike Brown.*

"Walter Johnson Base Ball Game." Walter Johnson Base Ball Games, Washington, D.C. The pieces have Johnson's picture on them. *Courtesy of Mike Brown.*

Base Ball Game, McLoughlin Bros., New York, copyright 1897.
The box and gameboard of this early game are lithographed on
cardboard. 7.25″ x 7.25″. *From the Kashmanian Collection.*

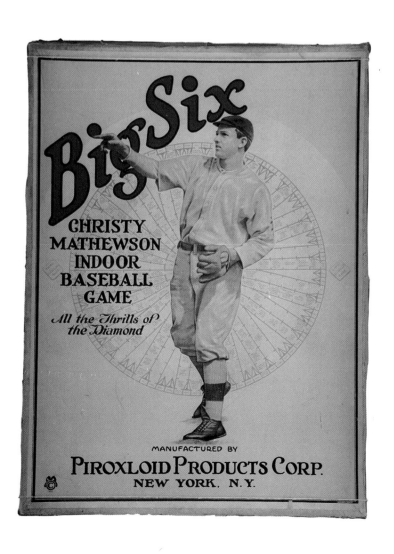

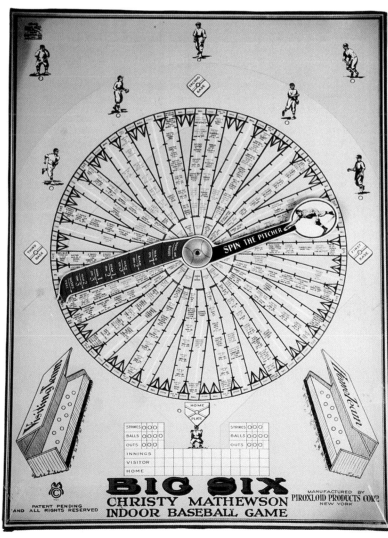

"Christy Mathewson Big Six Indoor Baseball Game." Piroxloid
Products Corp, New York, 1922. 23″ x 16.75″. *Courtesy of Mike
Brown and Ted Patterson.*

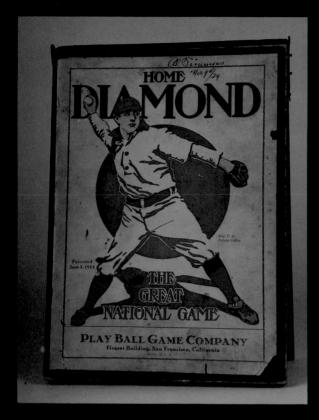

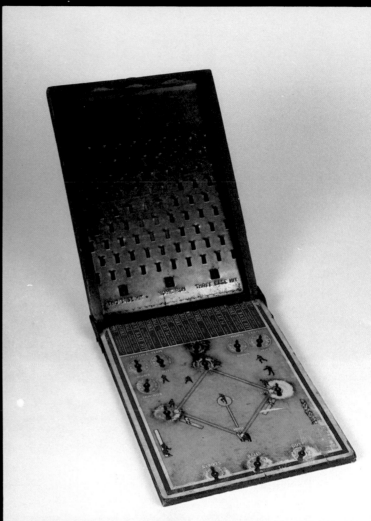

"Home Diamond, The Great National Game," Play Ball Game Company, San Francisco. Wood and metal, with paper labels, c. 1929. *Courtesy of Mike Brown.*

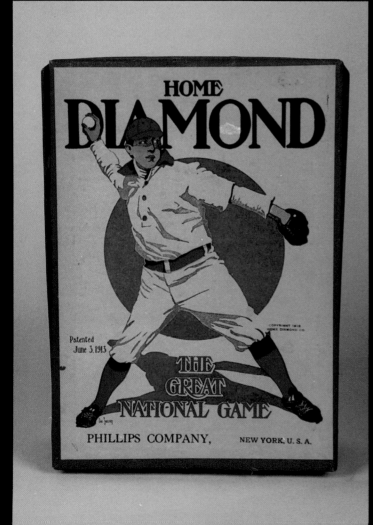

"Home Diamond," cardboard, Philips Company, New York. *Courtesy of Mike Brown.*

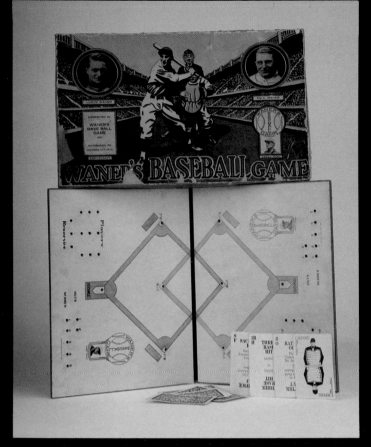

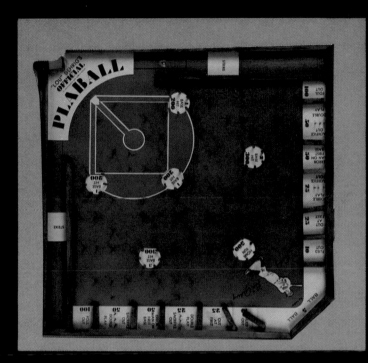

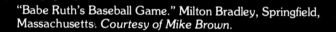

"Waner's Base Ball Game," Paul and Lloyd Waner. Distributed by Waner's Base Ball Game Inc., Pittsburgh, Pennsylvania, Oklahoma City, Oklahoma. Box: 14.5" x 10"; board: 18" x 12". *From the Kashmanian Collection.*

"Babe Ruth's Baseball Game." Milton Bradley, Springfield, Massachusetts. *Courtesy of Mike Brown.*

"Lou Gehrig" board game, Rich Illinois Mfg. Co., Morrison, Illinois c. 1930. *Courtesy of Mike Brown.*

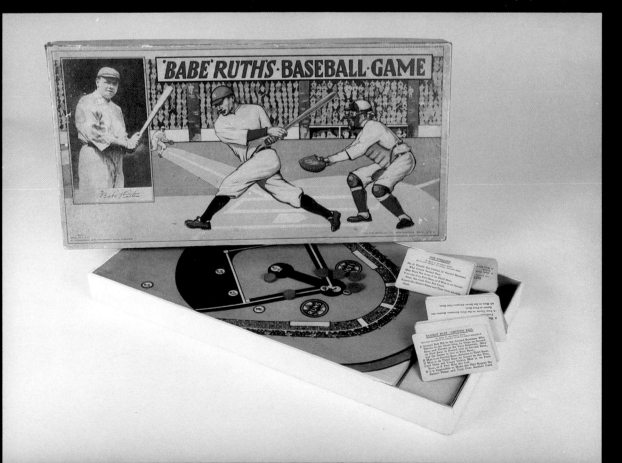

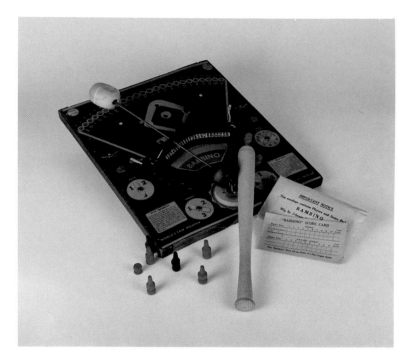

"Bambino" board game, manufactured by Johnson Store Equipment Co., Elgin, Illinois, 1933. Made for the World's Fair. *Courtesy of Mike Brown.*

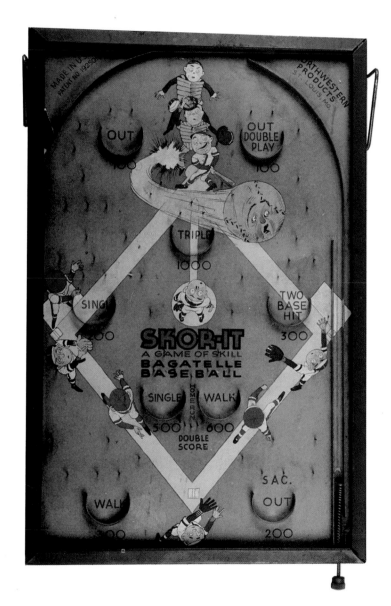

"Skor-it Bagatelle Baseball," Northwestern Products, St. Louis. 17″ x 11″. *Courtesy of Mike Brown.*

The original "Strike 3″ game by Carl Hubbell, Tone Products Corporation of America, New York City, c. 1939. *Courtesy of Mike Brown.*

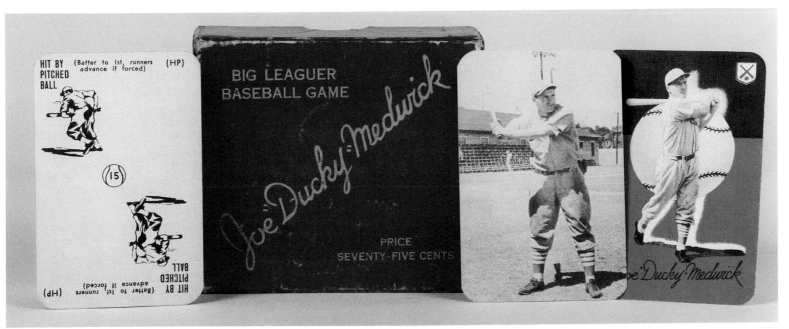

"Joe 'Ducky' Medwick Big Leaguer Base Ball Game," Johnston-Breir Co., St. Louis, 1939. *Courtesy of Mike Brown.*

"Big League Base Ball" card game, Whitman Publishing, 1939. *Courtesy of Mike Brown.*

"Pro Baseball" game, c. 1940. Masonite, wood, and composition, 8.5" x 8.5" x 4". *Courtesy of Mike Brown.*

"Star Baseball Game," Copyright 1941, Wm. P. Ulrich, president of the Spokane Baseball Club. *Courtesy of Mike Brown.*

"Base Hit" board game. Games, Inc., New York, c. 1944. *Courtesy of Mike Brown.*

Box for the Bee-Gee Base Ball Dart Target. *Courtesy of Mike Brown.*

Folk art bagatelle baseball game. Wood and paint, 37" x 13". *Courtesy of Mike Brown.*

Four of a set of sixteen hand-painted game figures. Each has its own number on the back and front of the uniforms. Only four sets are known to be painted. 1.5". *Courtesy of Mike Brown.*

Game piece, .75". *Courtesy of Mike Brown.*

Two-sided lead figures, c. 1910s. 2". *Courtesy of Mike Brown.*

Three dimensional Barclay lead figure, c. 1929. 1.75". *Courtesy of Mike Brown.*

Cast lead figures, raw and polished. Probably made in Pennsylvania, c. 1930s. 3". *Courtesy of Mike Brown.*

Cast players, c. 1930s. 3". *Courtesy of Mike Brown.*

Set of 19 lead players and umpire. Hand-painted New York and
Pittsburgh teams, circa 1920s. 1.5″-2.75″. *Courtesy of Mike Brown.*

Gray Iron's unissued test casting set, c. 1930. 1.5″. *Courtesy of Mike Brown.*

Auburn rubber figures, c. 1940s. 2.5″ x 3″. *Courtesy of Mike Brown.*

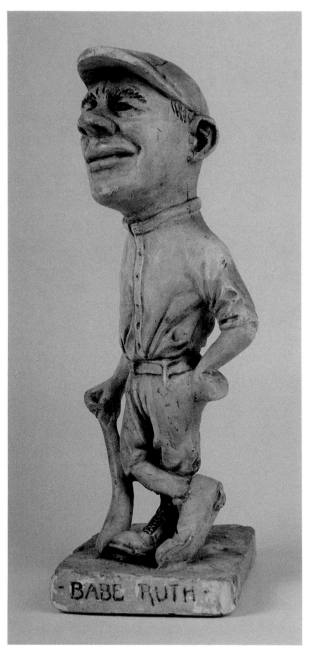

Babe Ruth statue from 1916. *Courtesy of Ted Patterson.*

Cast iron baseball still banks. The bank on the left screws from the front with a square nut on the back, the others screw from the back. 5.75". *Courtesy of Mike Brown.*

Smiley doll, composition and wire. Ideal Doll, U.S.A., c. 1930s. *Courtesy of Mike Brown.*

Bisque Mickey baseball players, four of six, Walt E. Disney, c. 1934. 3.25". *Courtesy of Mike Brown.*

Chalk nodder candy containers from occupied Germany, c. 1945.
6". *Courtesy of Mike Brown.*

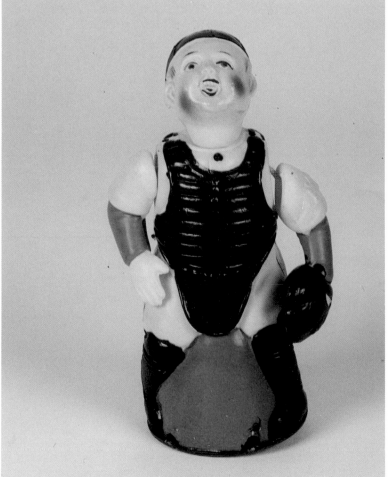

Bill Dickey Catcher, celluloid catcher windup toy. Occupied Japan,
5" x 2". *Courtesy of Mike Brown.*

"Home Run King" tin toy, Selrite Products Inc., New York, New York, 1930. 7″ x 6.25″ x 3.5″. *Courtesy of Mike Brown.*

Hartland Baseball Stars box and three figures: Ted Williams, Ernie Banks, and Stan Musial. *Courtesy of Ted Patterson.*

"Sensational Baseball Bank Game," 1943. It advertises Sealtest
Dairy Products. *Courtesy of Mike Brown.*

Wartime bat-shaped fan, opened when
allies invaded. *Courtesy of Mike Brown.*

"Fun-Go-Kat," early game, c. 1900. Wood, 5.25" x 12" x 5".
*Courtesy of Mike Brown.*

# Chapter 6
# *Baseball for Sale*

Baseball has been a favorite theme of advertisers, beginning in the late 1800s. Then, as now, companies looked for publicly recognized people to endorse their products. They wished to have their product seen as a kind of link between the consumer and the star, the implication being that if one used the product they would have the same kind of success.

Before the Civil War most products were more or less generic and sold in bulk. If you went to the general store for tobacco, you would receive whatever kind the storekeeper happened to have on the shelf. The same was true of whiskey, soap, sugar, flour, and practically every other kind of product.

The exceptions to this were so-called patent medicines. As early as 1708, an English medicine called *Daffy's Elixir Salutis* was advertised in a Boston newspaper. It soon was followed by countless "magic" cures. Every pharmacist dreamed of finding a formula that would bear his name...and make him rich.

Other products soon joined the trend toward brand names and the revolution in marketing and packaging spread. Tobacco was at the forefront of the movement, and tobacco

**Tobacco**

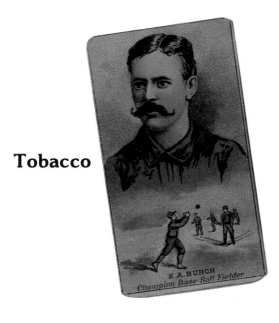

"E.A. Burch, Champion Base Ball Fielder." W.S. Kimball & Co's Cigarettes "Champions of Games and Sports" series, 1887. Ernie (Earnest W.) Burch played for Brooklyn of the American Association in 1887. 1.5″ x 2.75″. *From the Kashmanian Collection.*

"Dell Darling, Champion Base Ball Catcher." W. S. Kimball & Co.'s Cigarettes "Champions of Games and Sports" series, 1887. Darling played for the Chicago National League team in 1887. 1.5″ x 2.75″. *From the Kashmanian Collection.*

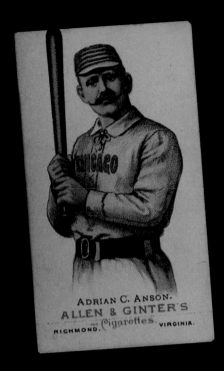

Adrian C. Anson, Chicago. Allen and Ginter Cigarettes, "The World's Champions" Series One, 1888. *From the Kashmanian Collection.*

Chas. W. Bennett, Detroit. Allen and Ginter Cigarettes, "The World's Champions" Series One, 1888. *From the Kashmanian Collection.*

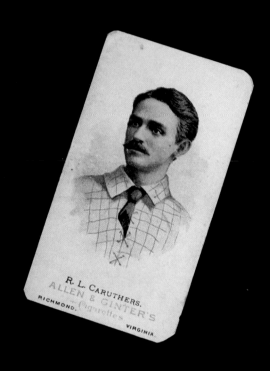

Allen & Ginter card of R.L. Caruthers. *From the Kashmanian Collection.*

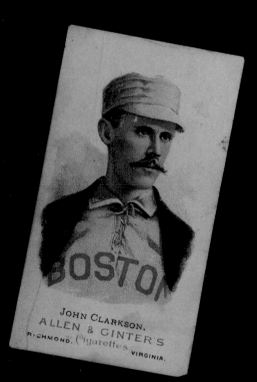

John Clarkson, Boston. Allen and Ginter Cigarettes, "The World's Champions" Series One, 1888. Hall of Fame, 1963. *From the Kashmanian Collection.*

companies were soon experimenting with literally thousands of names and designs looking for the one that would catch the public eye and establish a niche for itself.

In addition to a strong name, the early advertisers were quick to realize that image was an important factor in sales. They needed someone who was easily identified, had a respected, esteemed public persona, and was trusted to tell the truth. Who better to fill this bill than the baseball player? In growing numbers generic baseball images began to appear on tobacco tins and cigar box labels. Teams would lend their names to products. Players appeared on everything from cigar bands to trolley posters. From Fred Pfeffer Cigars to Bo Jackson in Nikes, the trend has continued into the present.

There was little thought given to the product being endorsed, and to our modern eye it is a little disconcerting to see baseball

Charles Comiskey, St. Louis. Allen and Ginter Cigarettes, "The World's Champions" Series One, 1888. Hall of Fame, 1939. *From the Kashmanian Collection.*

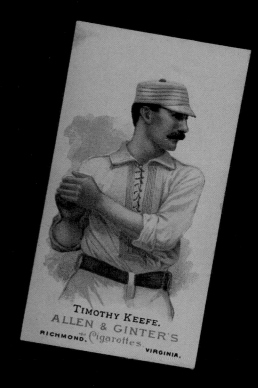

Timothy Keefe, New York. Allen and Ginter Cigarettes, "The World's Champions" Series One, 1888. Hall of Fame, 1964. *From the Kashmanian Collection.*

Capt. Jack Glasscock, Indianapolis. Allen and Ginter Cigarettes, "The World's Champions" Series One, 1888. *From the Kashmanian Collection.*

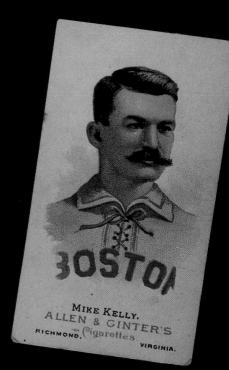

greats, the symbols of health and fitness, hawking cigarettes. In earlier times there were few such concerns. The early growth of baseball coincides with the a growing popularity of cigarettes in the late 19th century, and both found general acceptance among the men of the day.

A notable exception to this rule is Honus Wagner. His objection to having his image used on a cigarette card led to it being withdrawn from the market after only a few were released. The result is a card of legendary rarity and tremendous market value in the late 20th century.

Baseball advertising makes a wonderful addition to the collector's treasury. The colors and images are prime examples of the designer's and lithographer's art, making these items decorative as well as collectible.

Allen and Ginter Cigarettes, "The World's Champions" Series One, 1888. Mike "King" Kelly, Boston. Hall of Fame, 1945. *From the Kashmanian Collection.*

Joseph Mulvey. Allen and Ginter Cigarettes, "The World's Champions" Series One, 1888. *From the Kashmanian Collection.*

John M. Ward, New York Giants. Allen and Ginter Cigarettes, "The World's Champions" Series One, 1888. Hall of Fame, 1964. *From the Kashmanian Collection.*

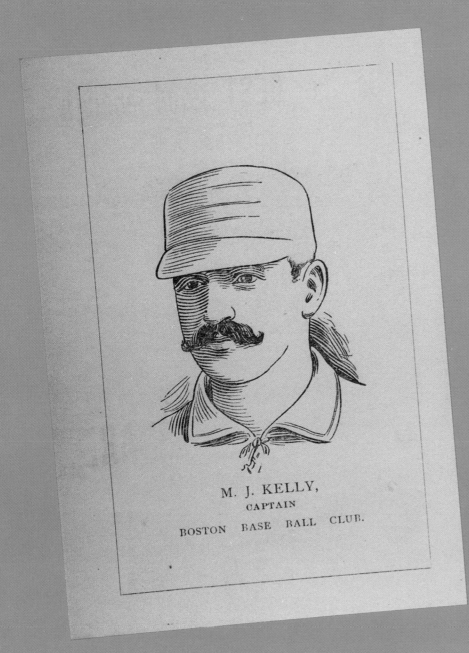

Adrian Anson, First Base, Chicago, Goodwin & Co. Champions Series, 1888. Advertising Old Judge & Gypsy Queen Cigarettes. Geo. S. Harris, Lithographers, Philadelphia. 2.75" x 1.5". *From the Kashmanian Collection.*

H.W.S. & Co. cigar card of M.J. "King" Kelly, captain, the Boston Base Ball Club, 1889. 4.5" x 3". *From the Kashmanian Collection.*

Jimmy Bannon, right fielder, Boston. Mayo's Cut Plug trade cards, 1895. Jimmy's brother, Tom, played for the New York National team, 1895-1896. *From the Kashmanian Collection.*

George Haddock, pitcher, Philadelphia. Mayo's Cut Plug trade cards, 1895. Played only part of the 1894 season with Philadelphia. *From the Kashmanian Collection.*

Herman Long, short stop, Boston. Mayo's Cut Plug trade cards, 1895. *From the Kashmanian Collection.*

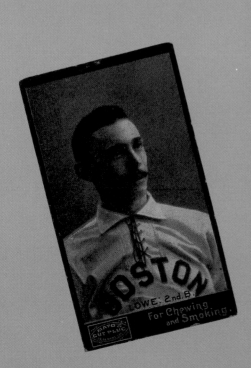

Bobby Lowe, second base, Boston. Mayo's Cut Plug trade cards, 1895. *From the Kashmanian Collection.*

Yale Murphy, short stop, New York. Mayo's Cut Plug trade cards, 1895. *From the Kashmanian Collection.*

*Hassan Cigarette triple folder, 1912. Charley O'Leary and Ty Cobb, Detroit American League. 2.25″ x 5.25″4. From the Kashmanian Collection.*

Hassan Cigarette triple folder, 1912. J. T. Meyers and Christy Mathewson, Giants. 2.25″ x 5.25″. *From the Kashmanian Collection.*

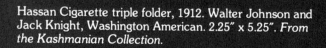

Hassan Cigarette triple folder, 1912. Walter Johnson and Jack Knight, Washington American. 2.25″ x 5.25″. *From the Kashmanian Collection.*

Hassan Cigarette triple folder, 1912. Jack Barry and "Home Run" Baker, Philadelphia American League. 2.25″ x 5.25″. *From the Kashmanian Collection.*

Hassan Cigarette triple folder, 1912. Smokey Joe Wood and Tris Speaker, Boston American League. 2.25″ x 5.25″. *From the Kashmanian Collection.*

108

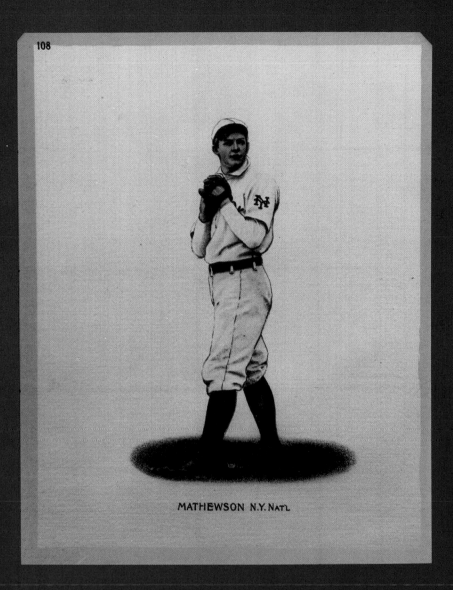

MATHEWSON N.Y. NAT'L

Christy Mathewson, New York National, tobacco silk, 1911. 7" x 9". *From the Kashmanian Collection.*

1911 pillow case with images of Walter Johnson of Washington, "Home Run" Baker of Philadelphia, Tris Speaker of Boston American, Ty Cobb of Detroit, and Christy Mathewson of New York National. *From the Kashmanian Collection.*

Sweet Caporal cigarette card featuring Nap Lajoie of Cleveland. 2.625" x 1.5". *From the Kashmanian Collection.*

1914 tobacco felts with Walter Johnson and Ty Cobb. 5.25" x 5.25". *From the Kashmanian Collection.*

Sovereign Cigarettes card featuring Joe Tinker of the Chicago Cubs. 2.625″ x 1.5″. *From the Kashmanian Collection.*

John J. "Johnny" Evers of the Chicago Cubs on this Cycle Cigarette card. Hall of Fame, 1946. 2.625″ x 1.5″. *From the Kashmanian Collection.*

A popular poem of the day made clear the threat that the combination of Tinker, Evers, and Chance posed to the hitters that faced them.

These are the saddest of possible words
Tinker to Evers to Chance.
Trio of bear Cubs and fleeter than birds,
Tinker to Evers to Chance.
Pricking our gonfalon bubble,
Making a Giant hit into trouble,
Words that are weighty with nothing but trouble,
Tinker to Evers to Chance.

Cycle Cigarettes card featuring Frank L. Chance of the Chicago Cubs, National League. 2.625″ x 1.5″. *From the Kashmanian Collection.*

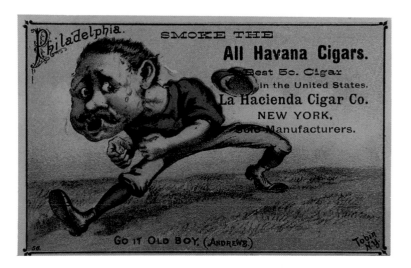

Tobin lithograph trade card, c. 1887. Advertising All Havana Cigars, La Hacienda Cigar Co., New York. Ed Andrews, Philadelphia. 4.5" x 3". *From the Kashmanian Collection.*

Chicago's Cap Anson on a Tobin lithograph, c. 1886. 3" x 4.5". *From the Kashmanian Collection.*

Tobin lithograph featuring a caricature of Dan Brouthers of Detroit. c. 1886. 3" x 4.5". No advertising. Hall of Fame, 1945. *From the Kashmanian Collection.*

Charlie Ferguson, Philadelphia. Tobin lithograph trade card, c. 1887. Advertising All Havana Cigars, La Hacienda Cigar Co., New York. 4.5" x 3". *From the Kashmanian Collection.*

Jack Glasscock, Indianapolis. Tobin lithograph trade card, c. 1887. Advertising All Havana Cigars, La Hacienda Cigar Co., New York. 4.5" x 3". *From the Kashmanian Collection.*

Paul Hines, Washington. Tobin lithograph trade card, c. 1887. Advertising All Havana Cigars, La Hacienda Cigar Co., New York. 4.5″ x 3″. *From the Kashmanian Collection.*

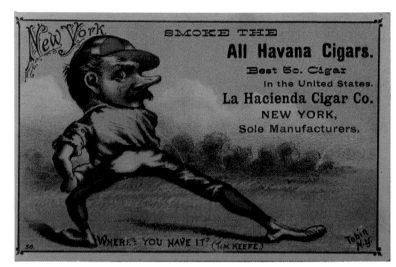

Tim Keefe, New York. Tobin lithograph trade card, c. 1887. Advertising All Havana Cigars, La Hacienda Cigar Co., New York. 4.5″ x 3″. Hall of Fame, 1964. *From the Kashmanian Collection.*

Mike "King" Kelly, Bosting (Boston). Tobin lithograph trade card, c. 1887. Advertising All Havana Cigars, La Hacienda Cigar Co., New York. 4.5″ x 3″. *From the Kashmanian Collection.*

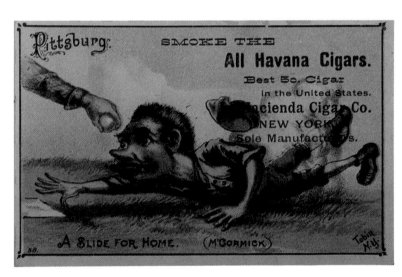

Jim McCormick, Pittsburgh. Tobin lithograph trade card, c. 1887. Advertising All Havana Cigars, La Hacienda Cigar Co., New York. 4.5″ x 3″. *From the Kashmanian Collection.*

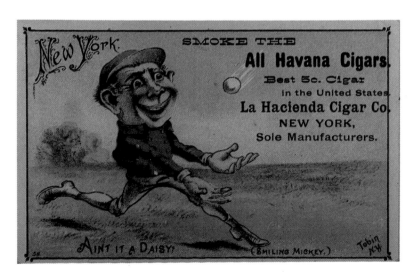

Smiling Mickey Welch, New York. Tobin lithograph trade card, c. 1887, Advertising All Havana Cigars, La Hacienda Cigar Co., New York. Hall of Fame, 1973. 4.5″ x 3″. *From the Kashmanian Collection.*

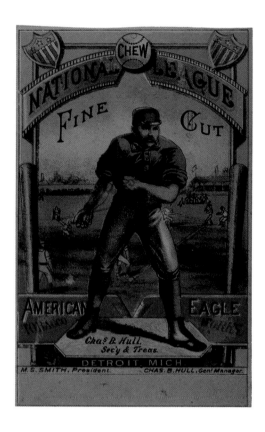

1880s tobacco trade card advertising National League Fine Cut made by the American Eagle Tobacco Works, Detroit. 3″ x 5″. *From the Kashmanian Collection.*

Allen & Ginter *Album of Champions* cover featuring John Montgomery Ward, c. 1888. Lindner, Eddy & Clauss, Lith., New York. *From the Kashmanian Collection.*

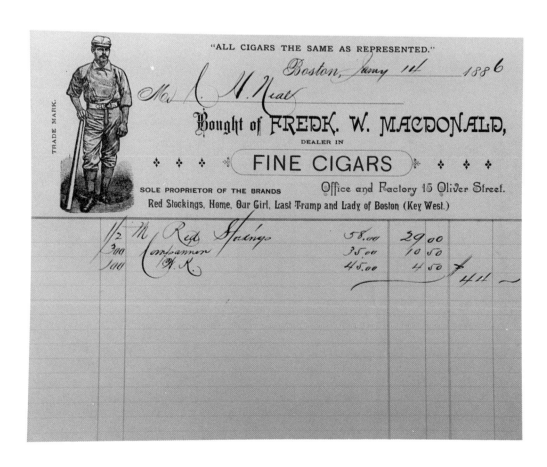

Billhead of Red Stockings Cigars, Boston, January 14, 1886. *From the Kashmanian Collection.*

"Goodwin Tobacco Base Ball Album: Champions 1888" with "Official League Ball" on cover.

The first page of the Goodwin Album with Mickey Welch, John Montgomery Ward, Buck Ewing, Tim Keefe all of New York.

Capt. Anson of Chicago on the second page of the Goodwin Album.

Jim O'Rourke, George Gore, Roger Connor, and Danny Richardson of New York on page three.

Mike Kelly of Boston on page four.

Old Judge and other Goodwin tobacco products are advertised on page five.

John Montgomery Ward appears again on page six in a close-up portrait.

Page Seven: Mike Slattery, Pat Murphy, Gil Hatfield, and Sam Crane of New York.

Charles Comiskey of the St. Louis Browns on  page eight.

Other New York players, Elmer Foster, Willard Brown, Bill George, and Mike Tiernan, on page nine.

On the last page of the Goodwin Album are Jim Mutrie, the New York manager, Cannonball Titcomb, Art Whitney, and the mascot. *From the Kashmanian Collection.*

Allen & Ginter poster featuring their Sports World Champions trade cards. Includes athletes from a variety of fields. The baseball players are William Ewing (catcher, New York), Charles H. Getzin (Detroit), John Morrill (1st, Boston), James Ryan (center field, Chicago), George F. Miller (catcher, Pittsburgh), James H. Fogerty (right field, Philadelphia), c. 1888. Second series poster. Printed by Lindner, Eddy & Clauss Litho, NY. 16″ x 28″. *From the Kashmanian Collection.*

Paper sign with outstanding color for Home Run Cigarettes, late 19th century. 17.5″ x 12″. Only known example. *Courtesy of Mark Rucker, Transcendental Graphics.*

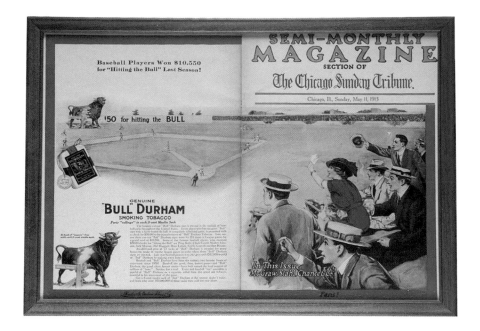

Front and back Pages of semi-monthly magazine of the *Chicago Tribune* featuring an advertisement for Bull Durham Tobacco merging with the front cover, May 11, 1913. The copy tells of an advertising scheme by Bull Durham that involved erecting bulls in various ball parks around the country, and awarding players $50 if they hit the bull. Among the 211 winners were Ping Bodie, Chick Gandil, Walter Johnson, Jack Murray, Hal Maggert, Hans Lobert, Gabby Cravath, and Ben Houser. 13″ x 19″. *Courtesy of Ted Patterson.*

Artist's proof of trolley car sign for Tuxedo Tobacco featuring Christy Mathewson, c. 1914. 22″ x 12″. *From the Kashmanian Collection.*

Tuxedo Tobacco trolley car sign with yellow background, featuring Christy Mathewson, c. 1914. 21″ x 11″. *From the Kashmanian Collection.*

Tuxedo Tobacco trolley car sign with John J. McGraw. 21″ x 11″. *From the Kashmanian Collection.*

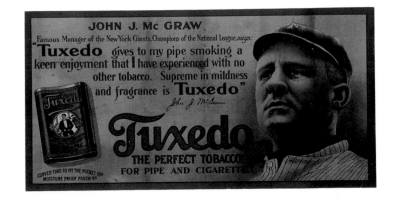

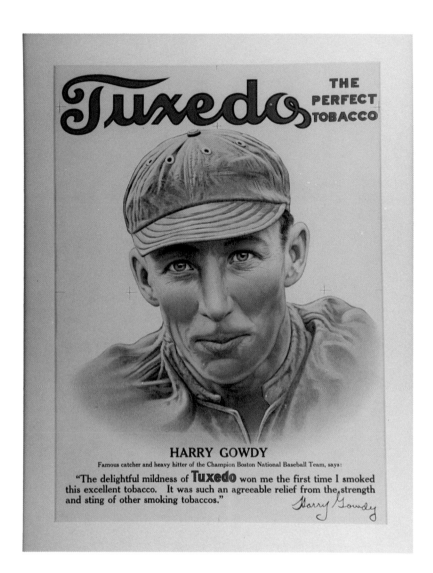

Artist's proof for a Tuxedo Tobacco advertisement with Harry Gowdy, 1915. The advertisement was made. Paper, 18.5″ x 13.5″. *Courtesy of Ted Patterson.*

Tuxedo Pipe Tobacco advertisement. On the left, top to bottom, are Fred Clarke, Miller Huggins, and Roger Bresnahan. On the right are Joe Tinker, Jimmy Archer, and Jack "Stuffy" McInnis. *Courtesy of Ted Patterson.*

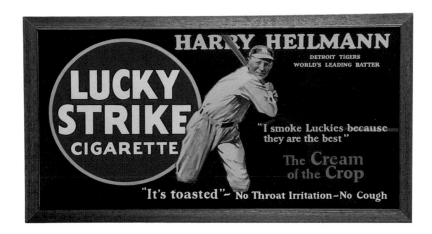

Lucky Strike Cigarette trolley car advertisement, c. 1927, with Harry Heilmann, Detroit Tigers, "World's leading batter." Paper, 10.5" x 20". *Courtesy of Ted Patterson.*

Lucky Strike trolley car sign, Tony Lazzeri, New York Yankees, c. 1928. 21" x 11". *From the Kashmanian Collection.*

Lucky Strike trolley car sign, Lloyd Waner, Pittsburgh Pirates, c. 1928. Lloyd had over 3,000 hits in his career. 21" x 11". *From the Kashmanian Collection.*

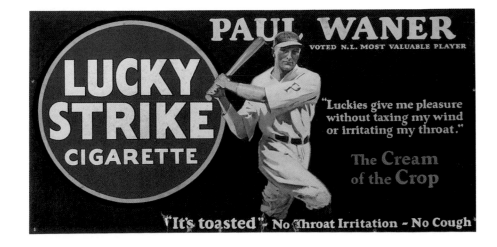

Lucky Strike trolley car sign, Paul Waner, Pittsburgh Pirates, c. 1928. 21" x 11". *From the Kashmanian Collection.*

Lucky Strike trolley car sign, Bob "Lefty" Grove, Philadelphia
Athletics, c. 1928. 21″ x 11″. *Courtesy of Ted Patterson.*

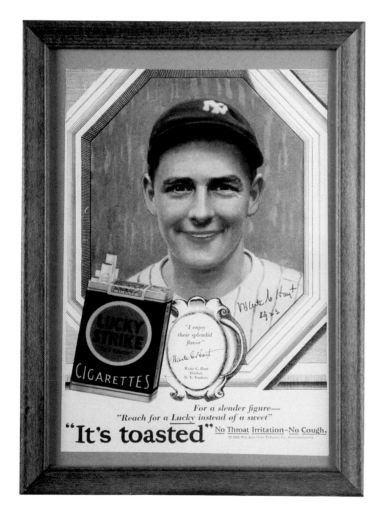

Lucky Strikes advertisement signed and dated by Waite Hoyt,
1923. 10.5″ x 7″. *Courtesy of Ted Patterson.*

Cardboard Mail Pouch poster, c. 1920s. The artist was J. Rozen.
34″ x 21.25″. *Courtesy of Ted Patterson.*

Lloyd Waner appears in this panel from a Lucky Strike tryptic advertisement, c. late 1920s. Paper, 34.5" x 15". *Courtesy of Ted Patterson.*

Die-cut Lucky Strikes sign in two parts, c. 1928-1929. This is Jim Bottomley. Cardboard, 36.75" x 17". *Courtesy of Ted Patterson.*

Lucky Strike Cigarettes advertisement with Lee Meadows, Pittsburgh Pirates, c. 1925. Cardboard. *Courtesy of Ted Patterson.*

This companion piece to the Jim Bottomley Lucky Strikes advertisement features his catcher, "Mickey" Cochrane. 28.5" x 18.5". *Courtesy of Ted Patterson.*

Cardboard sign for Red Jacket Tobacco, c. 1930s. 28″ x 22″. *Courtesy of Ted Patterson.*

Babe Ruth advertisement for Kaywoodie Pipes. Ray Morgan, artist. 24.5″ x 16″. *Courtesy of Ted Patterson.*

Die-cut cardboard sign for Union Leader Smoking Tobacco featuring Paul and Dizzy Dean, P. Lorillard Company, c. 1934. 42″ x 31″. *Courtesy of Ted Patterson.*

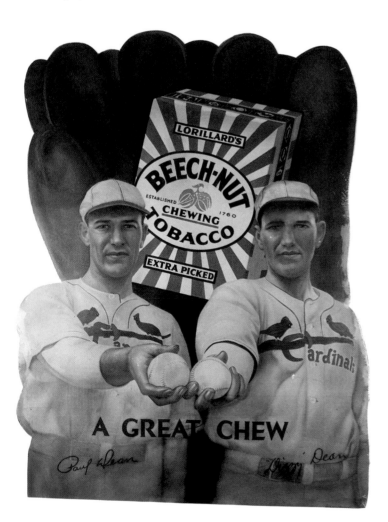

Die-cut Beech-Nut Chewing Tobacco sign with Paul and Dizzy Dean, P. Lorillard. Cardboard, 42″ x 31″. *Courtesy of Ted Patterson.*

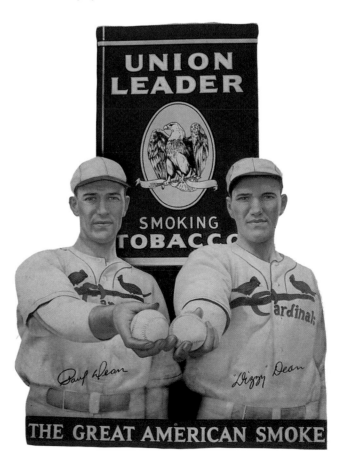

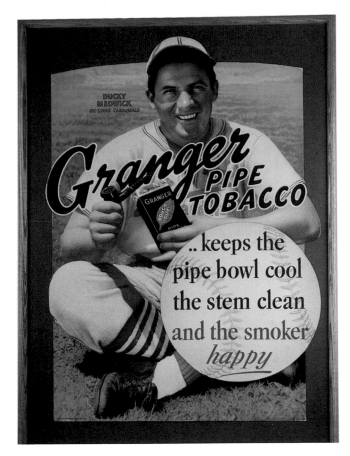

Die-cut cardboard Granger Pipe Tobacco sign with "Ducky" Medwick, St. Louis Cardinals. Liggett-Myers. 24″ x 34″. *From the Kashmanian Collection.*

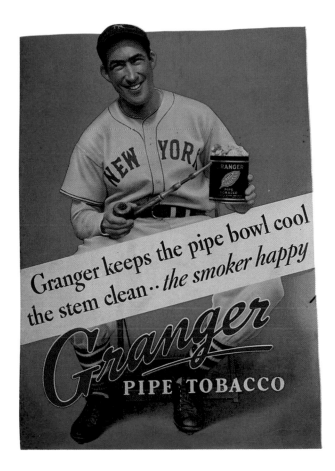

Granger Pipe Tobacco advertisement with Harry Danning, New York Giants, c. 1930s. Cardboard, 33.25″ x 22.75″. *Courtesy of Ted Patterson.*

Johnnie Mize, St. Louis Cardinals, in a Granger Pipe Tobacco advertisement, c. 1937. Paper, 20″ x 15″. *Courtesy of Ted Patterson.*

Bucky Harris on this Chesterfield Cigarettes poster, late 1940s. 21.5" x 21". *Courtesy of Ted Patterson.*

Chesterfield Cigarettes sign, c. 1948. Note that the National League players appear in uniforms, while the American League players are in street clothes. This is because of an American League rule. The players: Ted Williams, Stan Musial, Joe DiMaggio, Ewell Blackwell, Bucky Harris, and Bob Elliott. 21.5" x 21". *Courtesy of Ted Patterson.*

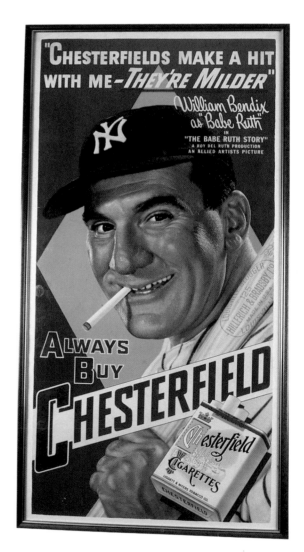

Chesterfield advertisement featuring Stan Musial. Liggett & Myers Tobacco Co., late 1940s. 21" x 22". *From the Kashmanian Collection.*

Chesterfield cigarette advertisement with William Bendix as Babe Ruth in "The Babe Ruth Story." Liggett & Myers Tobacco Co. 45" x 23". *Courtesy of Ted Patterson.*

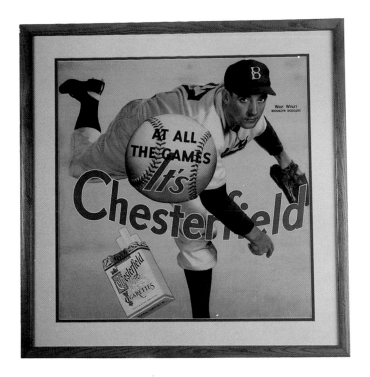

Chesterfield Cigarettes advertisement featuring Whitlow (Whit) Wyatt, Brooklyn. Paper, 21.5″ x 21″. *Courtesy of Ted Patterson.*

Chesterfield sign with Willie Mays, Liggett & Myers Tobacco Co. 21″ x 22″. Cardboard. *From the Kashmanian Collection.*

Chesterfield Cigarettes advertisement with Leo Durocher, from the late 1940s. Paper, 21.5″ x 22″. *Courtesy of Ted Patterson.*

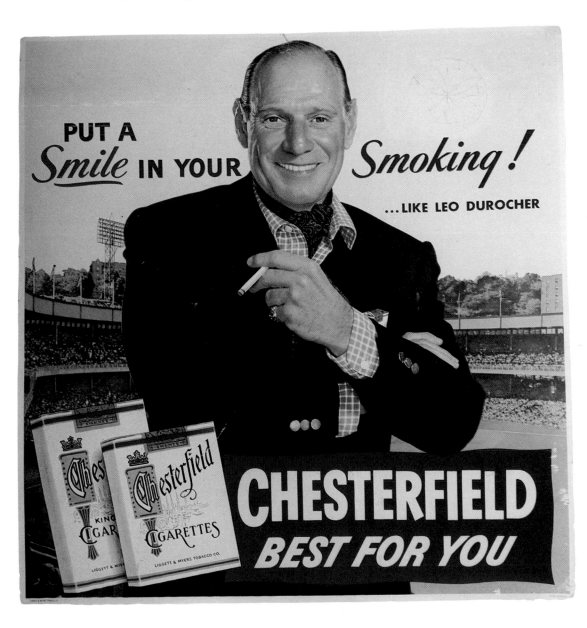

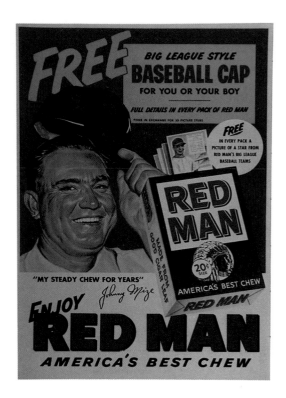

An Enos Slaughter baseball card is prominent in this advertisement for Red Man Chewing Tobacco. Paper, 15.5″ x 11″. *Courtesy of Ted Patterson.*

Red Man paper sign with Johnny Mize. 15.5″ x 11″. *Courtesy of Ted Patterson.*

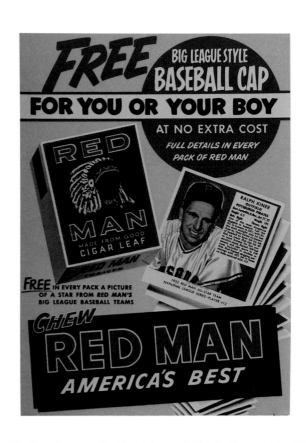

"Favorite Chewing Tobacco" paper sign with Nellie Fox. *Courtesy of Ted Patterson.*

1952 advertisement for Red Man with Ralph Kiner. 11″ x 15.5″. *From the Kashmanian Collection.*

Tobacco label, c. 1880, Banner Tobacco Co. 4″ x 3″. *From the Kashmanian Collection.*

Advertisement of Detroit Sluggers cigars, team photo of the Detroit Wolverines (National) Base Ball Club, 1887. The players: *standing*, Charlie Bennett, Dan Brouthers, Sam Thompson, Charlie Ganzell (sic), Larry Twichell (sic), Lady Baldwin; *seated*, Fatty Briody, Fred Dunlap, Bill Watkins, manager, Deacon White, Ned Hanlon, Bill Shindle, Charlie Getzein (sic); *on the floor*, Jack Rowe, Stump Weidman, Hardy Richardson. Photo taken by Tomlinson, Woodward Ave., Detroit. 10″ x 8″. *From the Kashmanian Collection.*

This "Hey Yea, Get A Lead" 5 Cent Cigar sign featuring Hughie Jennings, Detroit. *Courtesy of Ted Patterson.*

This cigar box label includes the image of William "Buck" Ewing, New York Giants, c. 1885-90. By O.L. Schwencke, Lith. New York. 7.25″ x 6″. *From the Kashmanian Collection.*

Sporting Times cigar label, 1888, New York Giants, National League champions. The players: *by the numbers, roughly left to right,* Cannonball Titcomb, Tim Keefe, Art Whitney, Mike Slattery, Monte Ward, Danny Richardson, Elmer Foster, Mickey Welch, Jim Mutrie, manager, Sam Crane, Bill George, Buck Ewing, Roger Connor, Gil Hatfield, George Gore, Jim O'Rourke, Mike Tiernan, Pat Murphy, Willard Brown. 7.5″ x 4.5″. *From the Kashmanian Collection.*

"Our Nine" cigar box label, c. 1875-80. Lithograph by Heppenheimer & Maurer, 22 & 24 N. William St. NY. 4.25″ x 4.25″. *From the Kashmanian Collection.*

Red Stockings cigar box. Holderer & MacDonald Mfgrs., Boston, Massachusetts, 1898. Lithographed paper on wood. 5.5″ x 6.5″ x 5.5″. *From the Kashmanian Collection.*

Red Stockings cigar box, named after the Boston Base Ball Club, Holderer & MacDonald Mfgrs. Red Stockings, Boston, Mass. 1901. Lithographed paper on wood. 6.5″ x 5.5″ x 5.25″. *From the Kashmanian Collection.*

Good Hit cigar box. Manufactured by S. Klobedanz, Waterbury, Connecticut. Paper on wood. 8″ x 5″ x 2.25″. *From the Kashmanian Collection.*

"Speedy Curves" cigar box. Paper on wood. 8.5″ x 5.25″ x 4″. *From the Kashmanian Collection.*

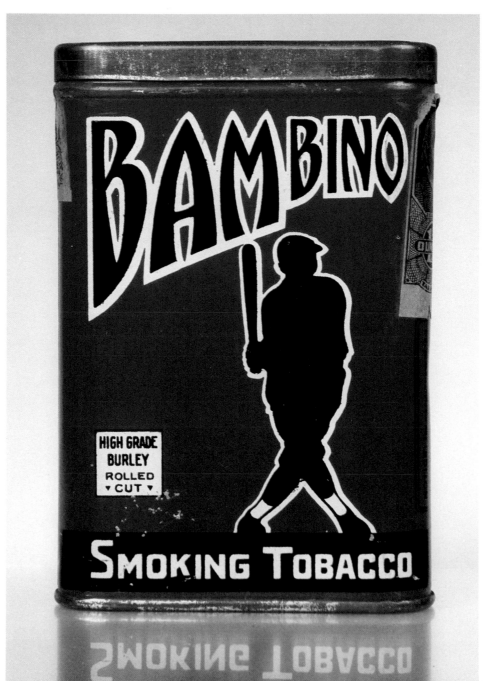

**Bambino** Smoking Tobacco pocket tin playing upon Babe Ruth's nickname and silhouette. Bailey Bros., Winston-Salem, North Carolina. 4.5″ x 3″ x 1″. *Courtesy of Dennis O'Brien and George Goehring.*

Lucky Curve Plug Cut Tobacco tin, Lovell-Buffington Tobacco Co., Covington, Kentucky. 4.25″ x 4.5″ x 7″. *Courtesy of Mike Brown.*

Yankee Boy Plug Cut Tobacco, upright pocket tin. Scotten Dillon, Detroit, Michigan. *Courtesy of Mike Brown.*

Bat Chewing Tobacco tin, Rock City Tobacco Co. Limited, Quebec. 3″ x 7.25″ x 6.5″. *Courtesy of Mike Brown.*

Chicago Cubs Chewing Tobacco tin, Rock City Tobacco Co., Quebec. 4.25″ x 6.25″ x 4.25″. *Courtesy of Mike Brown.*

Chicago Cubs Chewing Tobacco tin, Rock City Tobacco Co., Quebec, 1936. 3.25″ x 6″. *Courtesy of Mike Brown.*

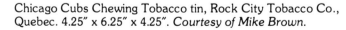

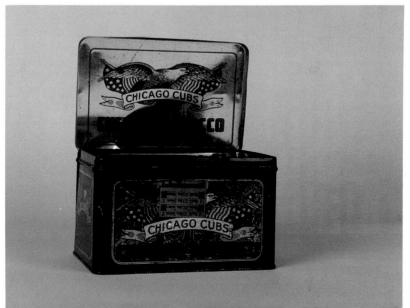

Pinch Hit Chewing Tobacco.
Paper, 5″ x 3.5″ x 1.5″.
*Courtesy of Mike Brown.*

Al Simmons cigar box. Simmons, "Milwaukee's
Favorite," played from 1924-1944 and is a Hall of
Famer. *Courtesy of Mike Brown.*

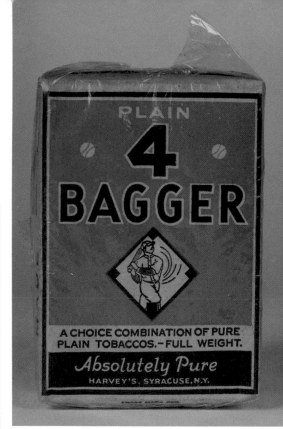

4 Bagger Tobacco, Harvey's, Syracuse,
New York. Paper, 5″ x 3.5″ x 1.5″.
*Courtesy of Mike Brown.*

Pfeffer's Hit Cigar band, F. Pfeffer Co., Chicago.
Features Fred Pfeffer, Chicago National League. 2.75″.
*From the Kashmanian Collection.*

Joe Tinker cigar box, Pennsylvania. Wood with paper
label. 8.5″ x 5.5″ x 2.25″. *From the Kashmanian
Collection.*

Jake Daubert Cigar band. Daubert played from 1910 to
1924, first for Brooklyn then Cincinnati. 2.75″ long.
*From the Kashmanian Collection.*

Federal League Cigar band. 2.75″. *From the
Kashmanian Collection.*

# Alcohol

"Four Balls" whiskey flask, c. 1870s. 5.75″ x 3″. *From the Kashmanian Collection.*

Match safe advertising West Side Brewery Company, Mundus Beer, Detroit on one side and the 1907-1908 Detroit Tigers, American League Champions for both years, on the other. The players: *top row* Sam Crawford, Ed Willett, George Winter, George Mullin, Charlie O'Leary, Ed Killian; *second row* , Ty Cobb, Wild Bill Donovan, Germany Schaefer, Red Killifer (sic?), Donie Bush; *middle row* , Navin, president, Hughie Jennings, manager; *fourth row* , Matty McIntyre, Oscar Stanage, George Moriarity, Claude Rossman, Davy Jones; *bottom row* , Heinie Beckendorf, George Suggs, Ralph Works, Ed Summers, Boss Schmidt, Elijah Jones. Celluloid and tin, 2.75″. Cruver Mfg. Co., Chicago. *From the Kashmanian Collection.*

Whiskey label, Federal League Bourbon Whiskey, c. 1914. 4.5″ x 5″. *From the Kashmanian Collection.*

Photo of Lewis Hack Wilson, with facsimile autograph, 1931. Compliments of Blue Ribbon Malt. 5″ x 7″. *From the Kashmanian Collection.*

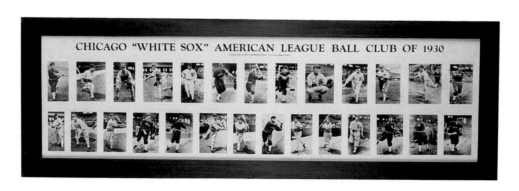

Photo poster of the Chicago "White Sox" American League Ball
Club of 1930, compliments of Blue Ribbon Malt. 11″ x 37.5″.
*Courtesy of Ted Patterson.*

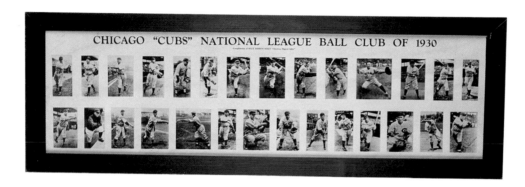

Photo poster of the Chicago "Cubs" National League Ball Club of
1930, compliments of Blue Ribbon Malt. 11″ x 37.5″. *Courtesy of
Ted Patterson.*

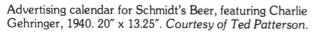

Advertising calendar for Schmidt's Beer, featuring Charlie
Gehringer, 1940. 20″ x 13.25″. *Courtesy of Ted Patterson.*

Hull's Famous Beer advertisement with Frank "Spec" Shea,
"Baseball's Rookie of the Year," 1947. 13.5″ x 10″. *Courtesy of Ted
Patterson.*

Narragansett Ale & Lager self-standing advertisement with a generic Red Sox player and sportscaster, Curt Gowdy. The sign is in three dimensions with a moving bat (incomplete), pre-1954. *Courtesy of Ted Patterson.*

New York Yankees team picture advertising Ballantine Ale & Beer. 1954. 15.25″ x 17.25″. *From the Kashmanian Collection.*

Metal Blatz Beer advertising display. 17″ high x 18″ wide. *Courtesy of Ted Patterson.*

## Soft Drinks

Coca Cola advertisement from a newspaper or periodical, 10″ x 14″. The Cleveland team is on the field with Napoleon Lajoie facing the stands. He and Rube Waddell endorse the benefits of Coca Cola in the copy of the advertisement. *Courtesy of Ted Patterson.*

Coca Cola advertisements featuring "Home Run" Baker (left) and Joe Tinker (right), probably from a magazine. 14.5″ x 5″. *Courtesy of Ted Patterson.*

Coca Cola advertisement from a large magazine like Colliers, c. 1913. Features Miller Huggins, Eddie Collins, Connie Mack, Nixey Callahan, John McGraw. The swirling arrow was an early Coca Cola trademark. *Courtesy of Ted Patterson.*

Coca Cola Co. cardboard advertising sign featuring Ty Cobb, copyright 1947. 13″ x 15″. *From the Kashmanian Collection.*

Coca Cola counter sign with Phil Rizzuto (autographed), c. 1952. 12″ x 11″. *Courtesy of Ted Patterson.*

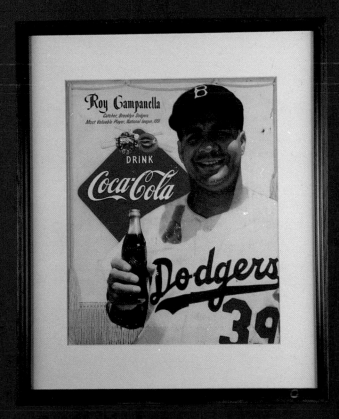

Coca Cola sign with Roy Campanella, copyright 1952. Paper, 11.5″ x 14.75″. *Courtesy of Ted Patterson.*

Counter sign for Moxie, c. 1920s—early 1930s. 13″ x 8.25″. *Courtesy of Ted Patterson.*

Autographed self-standing counter sign for Moxie with Ted Williams. Die-cut cardboard, c. 1953. 11.75″ x 15″. *Courtesy of Ted Patterson.*

Heavily reproduced in tin, this is the original cardboard counter sign for Ted's Creamy Root Beer, featuring Ted Williams. Autographed. 10″ x 15″. *Courtesy of Ted Patterson.*

Three dimensional self-standing Moxie sign with Ted Williams, c. 1950s. Cardboard, 8.5″ x 14″. Bottle for Moxie. *Courtesy of Ted Patterson.*

Ted Williams Moxie sign, c. 1950s. Cardboard, 31″ x 20″. *Courtesy of Ted Patterson.*

# Sweets

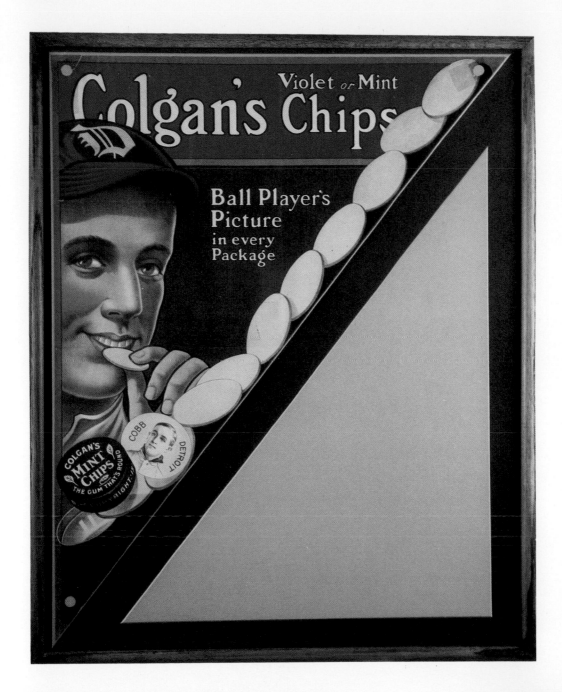

The top left triangle is the Colgan's Chips advertising poster featuring Ty Cobb, c. 1909-10. 20.5″ x 25″. *From the Kashmanian Collection.*

"Stars of the Diamond" card with picture of Ty Cobb, Detroit. Premium of Colgan's Violet Chips and Mint Chips. 1.5″ diameter. *From the Kashmanian Collection.*

Colgan's Mint Chips tin with card for Tris Speaker, Boston American, 1909-1910. Hall of Fame, 1937. 1.5″ x .625″. *From the Kashmanian Collection.*

Colgan's Chips "Stars of the Diamond" card for "Home Run" Baker of Philadelphia, American League, 1909-1910. 1.5″ in diameter. *From the Kashmanian Collection.*

Colgan's Violet and Mint Chips "Stars of the Diamond" series card for Joe Tinker of Chicago, National League. Hall of Fame, 1946. 1.5″ in diameter, c. 1909-1910. *From the Kashmanian Collection.*

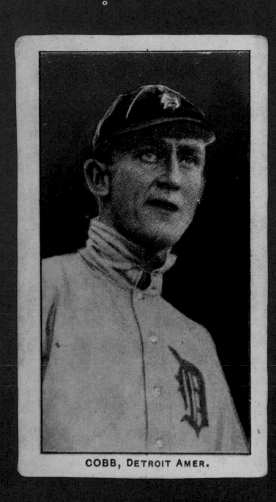

COBB, DETROIT AMER.

This card is one of a set of
25 BALL PLAYERS
Cards, as follows:

1. WAGNER, Pittsburg National
2. MADDOX, Pittsburg National
3. MERKLE, New York National
4. MORGAN, Athletics American
5. BENDER, Athletics American
6. KRAUSE, Athletics American
7. DEVLIN, New York National
8. McINTYRE, Detroit American
9. COBB, Detroit American
10. WILLETTS, Detroit American
11. CRAWFORD, Detroit Amer.
12. MATTHEWSON, N. Y. Nat'l
13. WILTSE, New York National
14. DOYLE, New York National
15. LEACH, Pittsburg National
16. LORD, Boston American
17. CICOTTE, Boston American
18. CARRIGAN, Boston American
19. WILLIS, Pittsburg National
20. EVERS, Chicago National
21. CHANCE, Chicago National
22. HOFFMAN, Chicago National
23. PLANK, Athletics American
24. COLLINS, Athletics American
25. REULBACH, Chicago Nat'l

Made by
PHILADELPHIA CARAMEL CO.
Camden, New Jersey

Premium featuring Ty Cobb, Detroit American, c. 1909. Included in candy by the Philadelphia Caramel Co., Camden, New Jersey. 2.75″ x 1.5″. *From the Kashmanian Collection.*

On the reverse of the Ty Cobb card is a list of other players in the series.

Original art work for the National Chicle Diamond Stars base ball cards, 1934. Jimmy Foxx. Hall of Fame, 1951. 5″ x 6″. *From the Kashmanian Collection.*

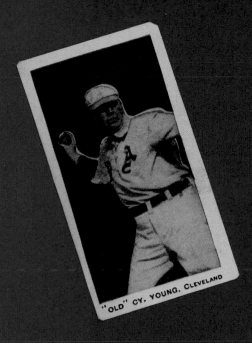

"Old" Cy Young, Cleveland, issued by George Close Co. and Blomes Chocolates, c. 1910. 2.75″ x 1.5″. *From the Kashmanian Collection.*

Mel Ott's Nation Chicle card original art work, 1934. 5″ x 6″. Hall of Fame, 1951. *From the Kashmanian Collection.*

Art work for National Chicle's Charlie Gehringer card, 1934. Hall of Fame, 1949. 5″ x 6″. *From the Kashmanian Collection.*

Dixie Cup premium, Bob Feller, Cleveland Indians, 1938. Hall of Fame, 1962. 10″ x 7″. *From the Kashmanian Collection.*

Dixie Cup premium, Jimmy Foxx, Boston Red Sox, 1938. 10″ x 7″. *From the Kashmanian Collection.*

Dixie Cup premium, 1937. Charles Gehringer, Detroit Tigers. 10″ x 7″. *From the Kashmanian Collection.*

Dixie Cup premium, Carl Hubbell, New York Giants, 1938. Hall of Fame, 1947. 10″ x 7″. *From the Kashmanian Collection.*

Dixie Cup premium, Wally Moses, Philadelphia Athletics, 1938. 10"
x 7". *From the Kashmanian Collection.*

Sports Kings Chewing Gum poster, "Stars & Champs of Today
and Yesterday," c. 1934. Baseball cards available included Ruth,
first card in the second row, and Cobb, third card in the second
row. Paper, 14.5" x 14". *Courtesy of Ted Patterson.*

Paper candy containers, Standard and Champion, Germany, c.
1910s *Courtesy of Mike Brown.*

Babe Ruth self-standing premium card advertised at left, 1933, Goudey Gum. 5.5" x 9". *From the Kashmanian Collection.*

A window sticker advertising a photographic print of Babe Ruth offered by Goudey Gum, 1933. 11.25" x 5.25". *From the Kashmanian Collection. From the Kashmanian Collection.*

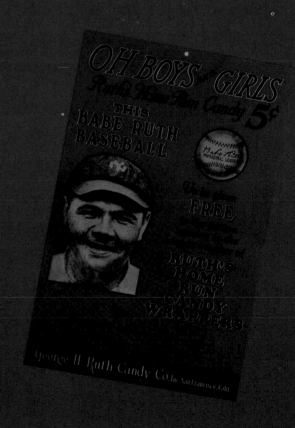

Babe Ruth hanging sign for the George H. Ruth Candy Co., San Francisco. Cardboard, 13" x 20". *From the Kashmanian Collection.*

This Topps group features original art work for their baseball cards (the top three and bottom three), the cards that use the art (on the sides), and a larger image from salesman's materials, 1953. Art work: 4.75″ x 3.75″; cards: 3.75″ x 2.75″; salesman's sample: 11″ x 7″. *Courtesy of Ted Patterson.*

Ted Williams Fleer card set, 1959. Box and cards. *Courtesy of Ted Patterson.*

## Food

Babe Ruth advertisement for Quaker Brand Puffed Rice. 20″ x 15.5″. *From the Kashmanian Collection.*

Quaker Brand Puffed Wheat or Rice sign with Babe Ruth, 1934. *Courtesy of Ted Patterson.*

1914 advertising blotter for Ferguson Bakery, with an offer for a felt pennant featuring Johnny Evers. 6″ x 4″. *From the Kashmanian Collection.*

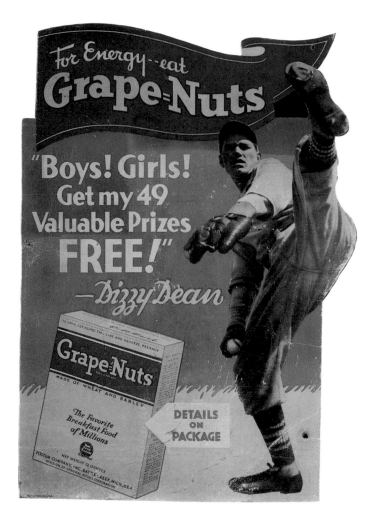

Die cut advertisement for Grape Nuts cereal with Dizzy Dean, 1937. The Postum Company, Battle Creek, Michigan. Paper, 31″ x 21″. *Courtesy of Ted Patterson.*

Old Judge Coffee advertising calendar, featuring the 1942 St. Louis Cardinals. David G. Evans Coffee Co., 1943. Paper, 14.5″ x 30″. *From the Kashmanian Collection.*

"The Pinch Hitter," a 1930s Mickey Mouse premium from Post Cereal. Die-cut paper, 4″ x 6″. *Courtesy of Mike Brown.*

Sunbeam Bread advertisement featuring the Oakland "Oaks," a Pacific Coast League team with many future major league players, 1953. 17" x 16.5". *Courtesy of Ted Patterson.*

Full color lithographed Wheaties advertisement featuring Joe Medwick, c. 1938. 10.5" x 13". *Courtesy of Ted Patterson.*

Wheaties advertisement featuring Joe DiMaggio (autographed) and other sports stars, 1937. Paper, 15.5" x 10.5". *Courtesy of Ted Patterson.*

Phil Rizzuto in this Wheaties sign, probably designed for use in the subway. Paper, 11″ x 21″. *Courtesy of Ted Patterson.*

Joe Page Wheaties advertisement, 1950. Approximately 20″ x 11″. *Courtesy of Ted Patterson.*

Post Cereal box panel, 1960, with Al Kaline, Detroit Tigers. Hall of Fame, 1980. *From the Kashmanian Collection.*

Crate label for Best Strike Apples, Mitchell Madesko, Watsonville, California. 9″ x 10″. *Courtesy of Ted Patterson.*

# Ball Games

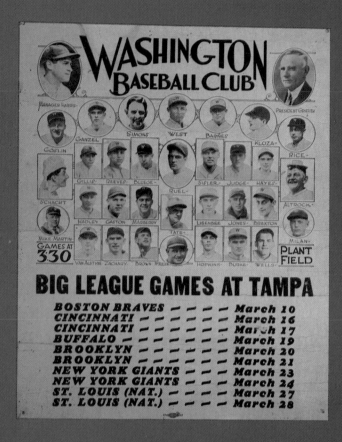

Flyers for Cardinals vs. Cubs and Cardinals vs. Giants games, c. 1937. Paper, 18"x 8". *Courtesy of Ted Patterson.*

Washington Senators spring training schedule. The players: *top row* , Bucky Harris, manager, Griffith, president; *2nd row* , Goose Goslin, Babe Ganzel, Simons, Sammy West, Red Barnes, Nap Kloza, Sam Rice; *3rd row*, Al Schact, Grant Gillis, Bobby Reeves, Ossie Bluege, Muddy Ruel, George Sisler, Joe Judge, Jackie Hayes, Nick Altrock; *4th row* , Mike Martin, Bump Hadley, Milt Gaston, Firpo Marberry, Benny Tate, Hod Lisenbee, Dick Jones, Garland Braxton, Clyde Milan; *bottom row* , Clay Van Alstyne, Tom Zachary, Lloyd Brown, Hugh McMullen, Paul Hopkins, Bobby Burke, Wells. Nick Altrock, a hero of the 1906 World Series, had by now teamed up Al Schact in a baseball clown act that appeared in ball parks around the country. Allied Printers. 1928. 22" x 28". *From the Kashmanian Collection.*

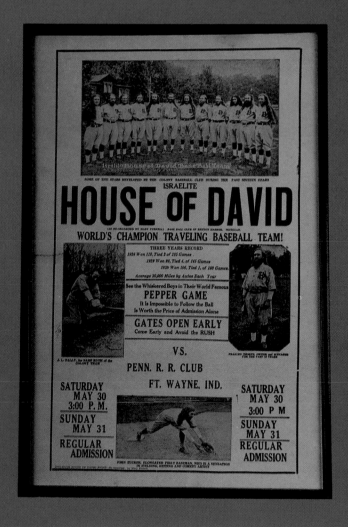

Poster for the Israelite House of David Baseball Team, at Benton Harbor, Michigan, c. 1931. Paper, 22" x 14". *Courtesy of Ted Patterson.*

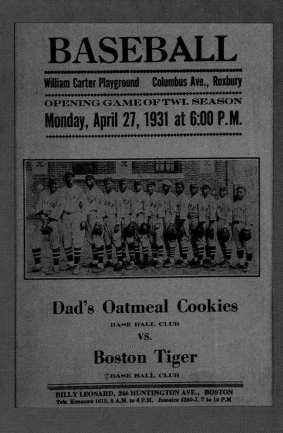

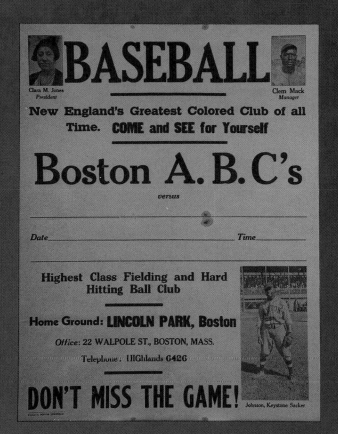

Broadside advertising a game between Dad's Oatmeal Cookies Base Ball Club and the Boston Tiger Base Ball Club. The team photo is of the Boston Tigers. April 27, 1931. *From the Kashmanian Collection.*

Advertisement for the Boston A.B.C.'s, Clara M. Jones, president. Clem Mack, manager. Johnson, Keystone Sacker. Printed by Boston Chronicle. 18″ x 24″. *From the Kashmanian Collection.*

Broadside honoring the Kansas City Monarchs, World Colored Champions, 1924. The image shows the first Colored World Series. 17″ x 11″. *From the Kashmanian Collection.*

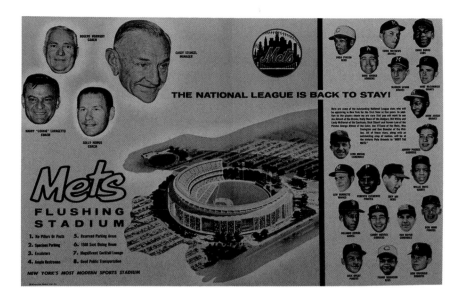

The inside of the Mets 1962 ticket brochure. *From the Kashmanian Collection.*

New York Mets ticket brochure for season ticket holders, 1962, the inaugural year of the Mets. 8.5" x 11", folded. *From the Kashmanian Collection.*

# Newspapers

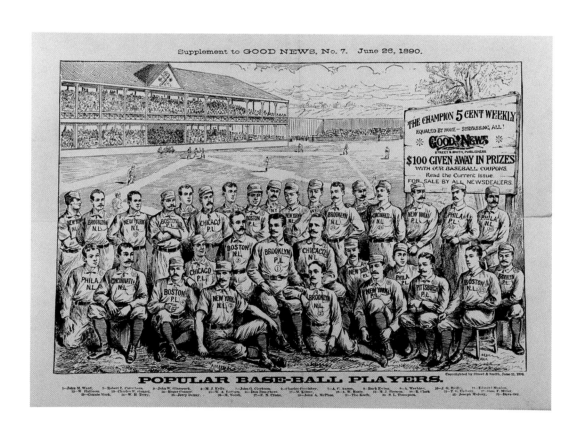

Supplement to the *Good News* newspaper, June 26, 1890, featuring the "Popular Base-Ball Players" of the day. This gives an interesting and rare view of the talent that went to the Players League. Although it lasted only one year, the outlaw league outdrew its two rivals in attendance with 980,887, compared to 813,678 for the National League and about 500,000 for the American Association. The players (N=National League; P=Players League): *standing, left to right,* Mickey Welsh (sic), New York N, Bob Clark, Brooklyn N, Mike Tiernan, New York N, Dan Brouthers, Boston P, Doggie Miller, Pittsburgh P, Arlie Latham, Chicago P, Connie Mack, Buffalo P, Matt Kilroy, Boston P, Cannonball Crane, New York P, Amos Rusie, New York N, Jerry Denny, New York, N, Adonis Terry, Brooklyn N, Gus Weyhing, Brooklyn P, John A. McPhee, Cincinnati N, Tim Keefe, New York P, Joseph Malvey, Philadelphia P, Sam Thompson, Philadelphia N; *seated ,* Tom Vickery, Philadelphia N, Long John Reilly, Cincinnati N, Mike "King" Kelly, Boston, P, Charles Comiskey, Chicago P, John W. Glasscock, New York N, John G. Clarkson, Boston, N, John Montgomery Ward, Brooklyn P, Cap Anson, Chicago N, Robert Caruthers, Brooklyn N, Roger Connor, New York P, Buck Ewing, New York P, Bill Hallman, Philadelphia P, Ned Hanlon, Pittsburgh P, Charlie Ganzel, Boston N, Dave Orr, Brooklyn P. Published by Street & Smith. 14" x 10.5". *From the Kashmanian Collection.*

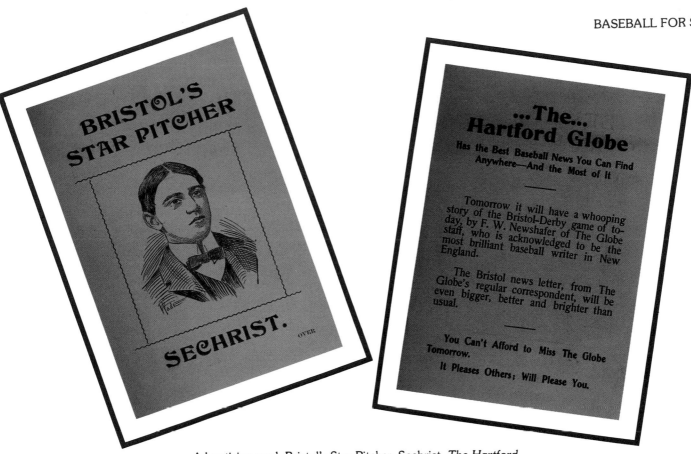

Advertising card, Bristol's Star Pitcher, Sechrist, *The Hartford Globe* . This may be Doc Sechrist who pitched in one game for the New York National team in 1899. 5.5″ x 3.5″. *From the Kashmanian Collection.*

Boston Red Sox 1910 calendar. Compliments of the *Boston American* newspaper. The players: *clockwise from top center* , Patsy Donovan, manager, Tris Speaker, Amby McConnell, Smokey Joe Wood, Jack Thoney, Larry Gardner, Ed Karger, Harry Smith, Bill Collins, Eddie Cicotte, Jake Stahl, Arrelanes, Harry Niles, Hap Myers, Duffy Lewis, Bill Carrigan, Harry Hooper, Charlie Hall, Heinie Wagner, Harry Lord. 14″ x 10″. *From the Kashmanian Collection.*

"What has become of Hal Chase?" cardboard sign issued by and advertising *The Sporting News* , c. 1918. The artist is Hixler. 14″ x 11″. *From the Kashmanian Collection.*

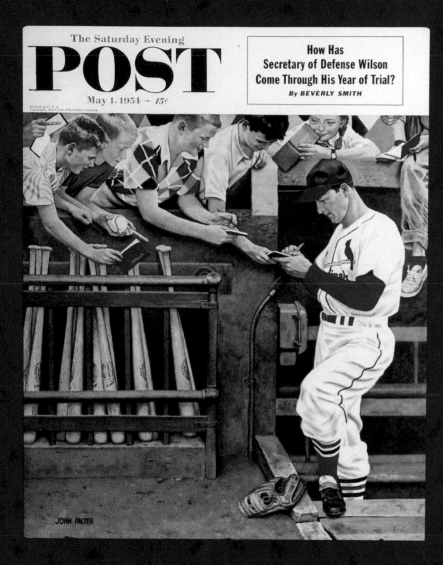

Window advertisement for the *Saturday Evening Post* , May 1, 1954, featuring Stan Musial signing autographs. Copyright, The Curtis Publishing Co.. John Falter, artist. *From the Kashmanian Collection.*

Color cabinet photo premium of Frank Chance, c. 1910, issued by *Sporting Life* . 6″ x 7.5″. *From the Kashmanian Collection.*

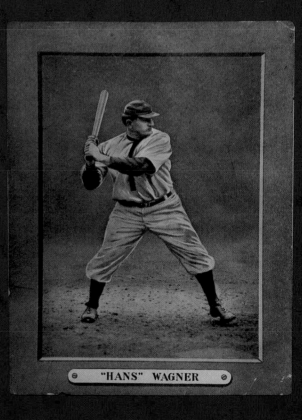

Color cabinet photo premium of "Hans" Wagner, premium, c. 1910, issued by *Sporting Life* . 6″ x 7.5″. Hall of Fame, 1936. *From the Kashmanian Collection.*

# Automobiles

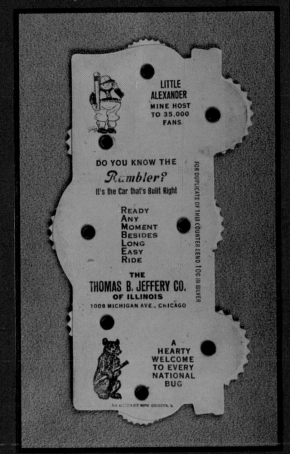

Chicago White Sox and Cubs celluloid score keeper, American Art Works, Coshocton, Ohio. c. 1915. 4″ x 2″. *Courtesy of Mike Brown.*

One of a series put out by Medcalf and Jim Bama, This calendar advertisement for Miller Buick features Casey Stengel. 1969. 23″ x 11″. *Courtesy of Ted Patterson.*

# Shaving Equipment

Magazine advertisement for Gillette featuring Donovan of Detroit, Chance of Chicago, Kling of Chicago, Wagner of Pittsburgh, and Jennings of Detroit, 1910. 8.25″ x 11″. *Courtesy of Ted Patterson.*

Trolley car sign for Gillette Safety Razor. Features Wild Bill Donovan of Detroit, Frank Chance of Chicago, Johnny Kling of Chicago, Honus Wagner of Pittsburgh, and Hughie Jennings of Detroit. 19″ x 9.5″. *From the Kashmanian Collection.*

Home Run razor blades box. The blades also have "Home Run" written on them. *Courtesy of Mike Brown.*

Gillette Tech Razor, World Series special, 1940. Has photos of Benny McCoy, Johnny Mize, and "Pepper" Martin. *Courtesy of Mike Brown.*

Gillette Shaving Cream, World Series special, 1941. *Courtesy of Mike Brown.*

Gillette Shaving Cream die-cut sign with John "Ziggy" Sears, National League Umpire. 36″ x 22″. *Courtesy of Ted Patterson.*

A die-cut for Gillette Razor Blades, sponsors of World Series, 1938. There is an endorsement from Red Rolfe in the lower right corner. 32″ x 23″. *Courtesy of Ted Patterson.*

# Motion Pictures

Lobby poster for "Raw Hide" with Lou Gehrig, 1938. Twentieth Century Fox. 11″ x 14″. *Courtesy of Ted Patterson.*

Theater poster for "The Kid from Cleveland," with the Cleveland Indians Baseball Team. Republic Pictures. *Courtesy of Ted Patterson.*

Lobby poster for "The Pride of the Yankees" with Gary Cooper and Babe Ruth. Copyright 1949 RKO Pictures. 11″ x 14″. *Courtesy of Ted Patterson.*

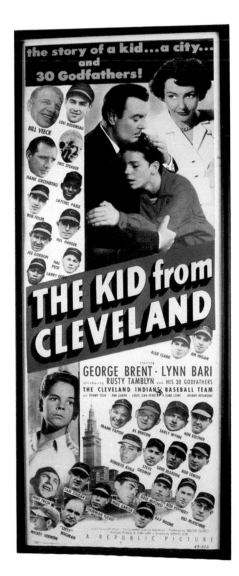

Lobby poster for "Roogie's Bump" starring Roy Campanella, Billy Loes, Russ Meyer, and Carl Erskine. Republic Pictures. 11″ x 14″. *Courtesy of Ted Patterson.*

Bookmark advertising the motion picture "The Jackie Robinson Story." Distributed by the New York Public Library. 8.5″ x 2.75″. *From the Kashmanian Collection.*

## Clothing

Joe Tinker is in a "Criterion" collar from Ide Silver Collars, Geo. P. Ide & Co., Makers, Troy, New York. Paper advertisement, 8.25″ x 11.25″. *From the Kashmanian Collection.*

Johnny Evers wears a "Caxton" in this advertisement for Ide Silver Collars, Geo. P. Ide & Co., Makers, Troy, New York. 8.25″ x 11.25″. *From the Kashmanian Collection.*

Advertising currency for Carver & Little, Merchant Tailors, Hanover, Pennsylvania. Marked "The National Base Ball League" on the front with a portrait of A.G. Spalding. The other side has members of the 1888-89 Chicago teams. Players portraits moving clockwise from the top center are Cap Anson, Tom Burns, Bob Pettit, Ned Williamson, Dell Darling, Tom Daily (sic), Silver Flint, Mark Baldwin, Marty Sullivan, George Van Haltren, ?,` and Fred Pfeffer 8″ x 3.5″. *From the Kashmanian Collection.*

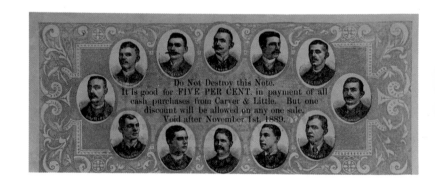

The "Berkeley" collar seems to suit "Home Run" Baker in this advertisement for Ide Silver Collars, Geo. P. Ide & Co., Makers, Troy, New York. 8.25″ x 11.25″. *From the Kashmanian Collection.*

Advertising pennants for Cravat's Ties with Joe Wood, Red Sox, Tris Speaker, Red Sox, Christy Mathewson, Giants, and "Home Run" Baker, Athletics. Each 8.25″ long. *From the Kashmanian Collection.*

"'Ty' Cobb and Geo. E. Keith" from a series of Walkover Shoe advertising posters, 1911. Photo by Richard W. Sears. 13.75″ x 10.75″. *Courtesy of Ted Patterson.*

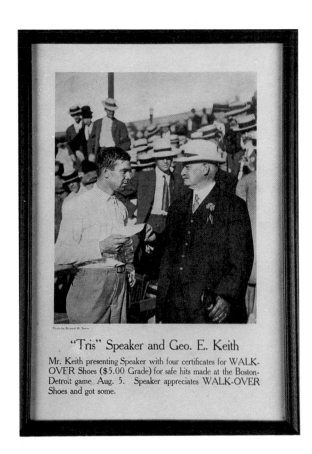

"'Tris' Speaker and Geo. E. Keith" from the series of Walkover Shoe advertisements, 1911. Photo by Richard W. Sears. 9″ x 13.5″. *Courtesy of Ted Patterson.*

33,904 People saw 32 pairs of "WALK-OVER" Shoes won at the Boston-Detroit Game, Aug. 5, 1911. The Geo. E. Keith Company had as their guests at the game 124 Superintendents, Foremen and Heads of Departments with the full "WALK-OVER" Band of 25 pieces.

A ballpark shot of the August 5, 1911 Boston-Detroit game from a series of Walkover Shoe advertisements. Photo taken with "Bell's Straight Working Camera." 10.25" x 21.5". *Courtesy of Ted Patterson.*

Another of the Walkover series of advertisements. This is the last year that the Huntington Avenue ball park was used by Boston. Fenway Park was opened in 1912. They game drew the largest crowd in the history of organized ball to that time: 33,904. 10.25" x 21.5". *Courtesy of Ted Patterson.*

This match striker features the 1912 Boston Red Sox in an advertisement for McMorrow's shoes, Boston. A.D. Ropes, Boston. 5" x 6.5". *From the Kashmanian Collection.*

The largest crowd ever in attendance in organized baseball, 33,904 people, were present at the Boston-Detroit Game, Aug. 5, 1911. A pair of "WALK-OVER" Shoes, ($5.00 Grade,) was given for every safe hit made by the players of either team. Altogether 32 certificates were presented.

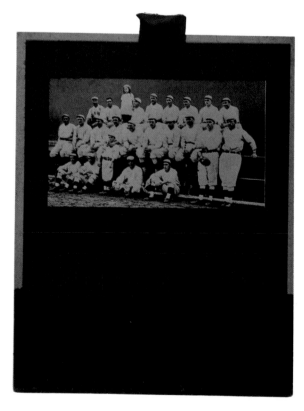

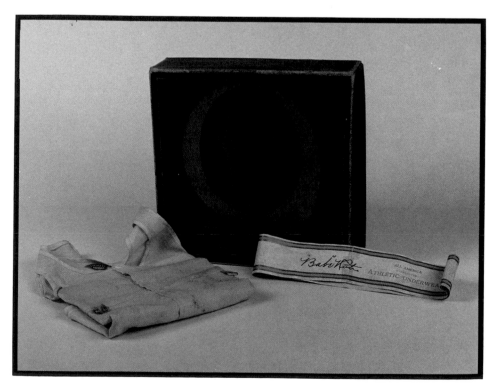

Babe Ruth Juniors Underwear for Boys with box, late 1920s. 10" x 10" x 3". *Courtesy of Ted Patterson.*

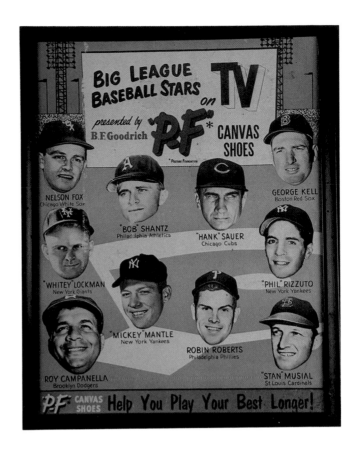

Clothing sample book, "The Victor and the Vanquished," featuring Eddie Collins, George Stallings, Connie Mack, Johnny Evers. Paper, 21″ x 14″. *Courtesy of Ted Patterson.*

"P.F." Canvas Shoes advertising sign, with pictures of major league stars, c. 1952. The players, Nellie Fox, Bob Shantz, Hank Sauer, George Kell, Whitey Lockman, Phil Rizzuto, Mickey Mantle, Robin Roberts, Roy Campanella, and Stan Musial. B.F. Goodrich Co. Paper, 25″ x 19″. *Courtesy of Ted Patterson.*

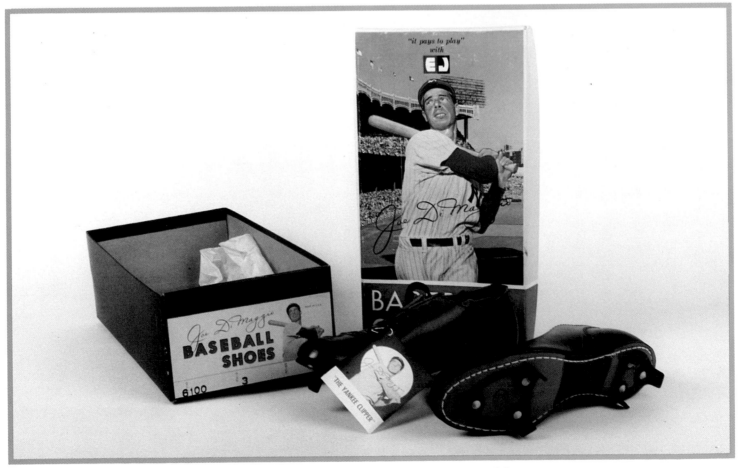

Joe DiMaggio Base Ball Shoes with box, c. 1949. Endicott Johnson Shoe Co., size 3, signed. *Courtesy of Ted Patterson.*

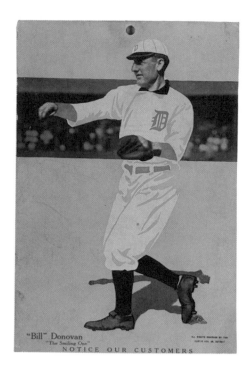

Advertising calendar top with "Bill" Donovan, for Hyatt Roller Bearings, c. 1909. The Curtis Advertising Co., Detroit. 4.25″ x 6.75″. *From the Kashmanian Collection.*

Advertising calendar top with "Donnie" (sic) Bush, "Just broke in, but all to the Good." The Curtis Advertising Co., Detroit, c. 1909. 4.25″ x 6.75″. *From the Kashmanian Collection.*

Advertising calendar top with "Sam" Crawford. "As 'Stable and Dependable' as our 'Universal Giant' Line and 'Wayne' Belting." Curtis Advertising Co., Detroit, c. 1909. 4.25″ x 6.75″. *From the Kashmanian Collection.*

The 1924 Pittsburgh Baseball Team is featured in this advertisement by and for Superior Engraving Co., Pittsburgh. The players: *top row*, Kiki Cuyler, May, Wilbur Cooper, Emil Yde, Glen Wright, Barney Dreyfuss, Bill McKechnie, Bill Hinchman, Pie Traynor, Chick (?) Fraser, Grover (?) Land, Jewel Ens; *middle row,* Mickey (?) Devine, Max Carey, Ray Kremer, Ray Steineder, Johnny Gooch, Charlie Grimm, Cliff Knox, Arnie Stone, Johnny Morrison; *bottom row*, Lee Meadows, Clyde Barnhart, Eppie Barnes, Rabbit Maranville, Eddie Moore, Johnny Rawlings, Del Lundgren, Carson Bigbee, Walter Schmidt, Walter Mueller. Paper, 6.5″ x 13.25″. *Courtesy of Ted Patterson.*

War bonds award, 1943. The players: *top row*, Bob Feller, Johnny Murphy, Charles Ruffing, Del Baker, Bob Johnson, Jimmy Foxx, Earl Averill, Rudy York; *2nd row,* Lefty Grove, Joe DiMaggio, Lou Gehrig, Lefty Gomez, Red Rolfe, Hank Greenberg; *3rd row,* Joe McCarthy, Johnny Allen, Arthur Fletcher, John Schulte, Buck Newsom; *bottom row*, Roger Cramer, Charlie Gehringer, Bill Dickey, Cecil Travis, Vernon Kennedy, Rick Ferrell, Joe Cronin, Buddy Lewis. 21″ x 12.5″. *From the Kashmanian Collection.*

This calendar for the Blue Palace Tea Shop and Hotel, Columbia, South Carolina was a Christmas giveaway. It features Jackie Robinson and a facsimile autograph. Copyright GAC, New York. 12″ x 15″. *Courtesy of Ted Patterson.*

Advertising calendar top with "Manager" Jennings, "Made a winner by eliminating friction. So can you by using 'Hyatt' Roller Bearings." Curtis Advertising Co., Detroit, c. 1909. 4.25″ x 6.75″. *From the Kashmanian Collection.*

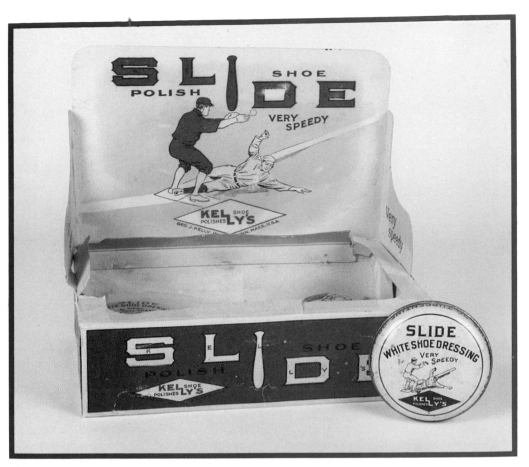

Kelly's Slide Shoe Polish counter dispenser and tin, George J. Kelly, Inc., Lynn, Massachusetts. 8″ x 9″ x 6″. *Courtesy of Mike Brown.*

# Other Advertising

Pepper Martin in this U.S. Deck Paint advertisement. The photograph is from the Elliot Photo Co. of New York. 16.5″ x 13.75″. *Courtesy of Ted Patterson.*

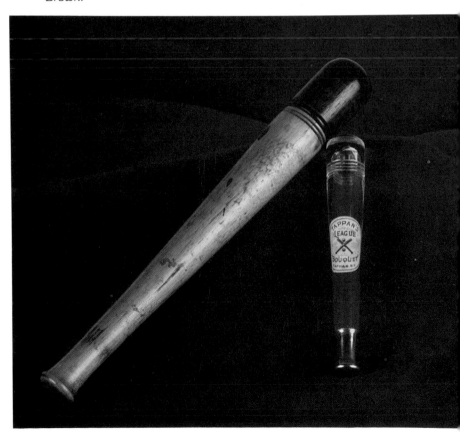

Cologne bottle with wooden holder. Tappan's League Bouquet, c. 1890-1900. Tappan, New York. The 6″ glass bottle fits in bat. *From the Kashmanian Collection.*

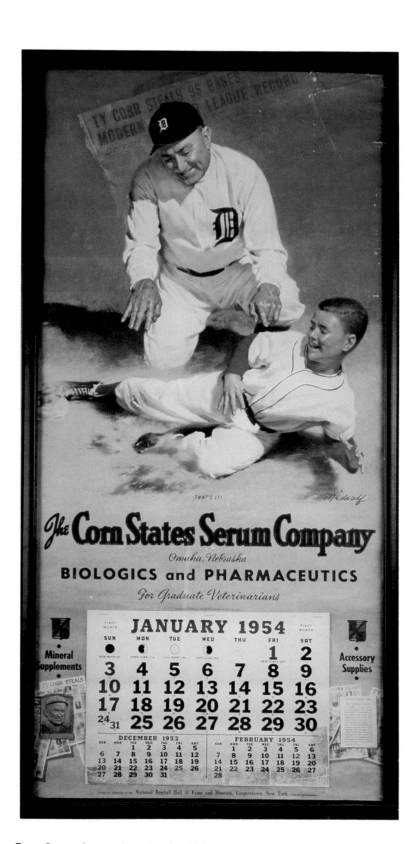

Corn States Serum Co., Omaha, Nebraska, 1954 calendar
advertisement with Ty Cobb. 33" x 16". *Courtesy of Ted
Patterson.*

# *Bibliography*

*Baseball Encyclopedia, The.* New York: Macmillan Publishing
Company, 1990.

Bock, Hal. *The Associated Press Pictorial History of Baseball.*
New York: Mallard Press, 1990.

Capano, Peter. *Baseball Collectibles.* West Chester, PA: Schiffer
Publishing, 1989.

Congdon-Martin, Douglas. *America for Sale: A Collector's Guide
to Antique Advertising.* West Chester, PA: Schiffer Publishing,
1991.

———*Drugstore & Soda Fountain Antiques.* West Chester, PA:
Schiffer Publishing, 1991.

——— *Tobacco Tins: A Collector's Guide.* West Chester, PA:
Schiffer Publishing, 1992.

Douglas, John A. *Sports Memorabilia.* Des Moines: Wallace-
Homestead Book Co., 1976.

Durso, Joseph. *Baseball and the American Dream.* St. Louis: The
Sporting News, 1986.

Goodrum, Charles & Helen Dalrymple. *Advertising in America:
The First 200 Years.* New York: Harry N. Abrams, Publishers,
1990.

Goldstein, Warren. *Playing for Keeps: A History of Early Baseball.*
Ithaca: Cornell University Press, 1989.

Holway, John B. *Blackball Stars: Negro League Pioneers.*
Westport, CT: Meckler Books, 1988.

Klamkin, Marian. *Old Sheet Music: A Pictorial History.* New
York: Hawthorn Books, Inc., 1975.

Kunhardt, Dorothy Meserve and Philip B. *Mathew Brady and His
World.* Alexandria, VA: Time-Life Books: 1977

Levy, Lester S. *Picture the Songs.* Baltimore: The John Hopkins
University Press, 1976.

McCulloch, Lou W. *Card Photographs: A Guide to their History
and Value.* West Chester, PA: Schiffer Publishing, 1981.

Raycraft, Don and Stew Salowitz. *Collector's Guide to Baseball
Memorabilia.* Paducah, KY: Collector Books, 1987.

Rust, Art, Jr. *"Get that Nigger Off the Field!"* New York,
Delacorte Press.

Schoor, Gene. *The History of the World Series.* New York:
William Morrow and Company, Inc., 1990.

Smith, Robert. *Baseball in America.* New York: Holt, Rinehart
and Winston, 1961.

Staff, Frank. *The Picture Postcard & Its Origins.* New York:
Frederick A. Praeger, Publishers, 1966.

Suehsdorf, A.D. *The Great American Baseball Scrapbook.* New
York: Rutledge Books, Inc., 1978.

Reidenbaugh, Lowell. *Baseball's Hall of Fame Cooperstown:
Where the Legends Live Forever.* New York: Arlington House,
Inc., 1986

# Index